Tools
for a Great
Marriage
DEVOTIONAL

Tools for a Great Marriage DEVOTIONAL

52 Devotional Dates for Building a Great Marriage

WILLIAM BATSON

WCBatson Consulting

Tools for Building Great Relationships

Somersworth, New Hampshire

*To all the couples who use this book,
may God richly bless your lives and marriages
with his abiding and abundant grace.*

AUTHOR'S NOTE

Using content from my first book, *Tools for a Great Marriage*, combined with new material, I created 52 Devotional Dates that invite God's presence into your marriage. Each devotional consists of a suggested Bible passage and devotional to be read aloud. In the Let's Talk About It section, there are two or three questions to stimulate some discussion. A written prayer, which you can read aloud, concludes the devotional time. At the back of the book (page 113), you will find several journal pages on which you can record your insights and decisions.

Tools for a Great Marriage Devotional is to be read in 52 separate sittings, once a week over a period of 12 months. A daily devotional time focused on your marriage can be challenging. For some it has led to failure and even guilt. I believe that a weekly Devotional Date focused on your marriage will be more profitable. The other six days can be spent doing general devotions.

I pray that this spiritual journey with your spouse will strengthen your marriage for years to come.

Devotional Date #1

All Scripture is inspired by God and is useful to teach us what is true and to make us realize what is wrong in our lives. It straightens us out and teaches us to do what is right. It is God's way of preparing us in every way, fully equipped for every good thing God wants us to do.

2 Timothy 3:16 (NLT)

. . . .

On an airplane somewhere over the northeastern part of the United States, the passenger next to me initiated a conversation. It was soon apparent that we had some striking differences in life experience. He had been married and divorced, was a recovering alcoholic, played in a funk music band, taught piano, and was on his way to a Stevie Wonder concert.

Our spirited conversation took more twists and turns than did the airplane that day. When he discovered I was a marriage educator, nothing hindered him from telling me about the lessons he learned from his past and present relationships.

His most profound statement related to something he tells his piano students, "Practice makes perfect, but if you practice wrong, you will be perfectly wrong."

Immediately, I thought of the couples who practice wrong relational skills repeatedly. They escalate arguments in order to intimidate and demean each other. They readily point out the flaws of loved ones and ignore their own serious deficiencies. Doing the same thing so many times and for so long, they become experts in being perfectly wrong. Practice is important, but my new friend taught me that the way we practice is much more fundamental to success.

Our relational tools and methods must be grounded in the counsel of God, who designed marriage. Otherwise, they lack the power to sustain a lasting and fulfilling relationship as God intended. The Word of God is foundational to building a marriage that is strong, durable, and lasting. It is an authoritative resource in teaching us how to get along with others. Just consider the following verses for example:

- *Be kind and compassionate to one another, forgiving each other, just as in Christ God forgave you. – Ephesians 4:32*

- *Don't grumble against each other, brothers, or you will be judged. The Judge is standing at the door! – James 5:9*

- *Do not lie to each other, since you have taken off your old self with its practices. – Colossians 3:9*

- *And let us consider how we may spur one another on toward love and good deeds. – Hebrews 10:24*

- *Love each other with genuine affection, and take delight in honoring each other. – Romans 12:10, NLT*

Imagine the kind of marriage you would have if you practiced these guidelines. It would be a great marriage!

Let's Talk About It:

1. How important is God's Word in your marriage?

2. How would your marriage relationship be stronger if you both practiced the guidelines mentioned in the Bible quotes above?

3. How can your spouse pray for you in the coming week?

Prayer:

Thank you, Father, for your enduring and encouraging Word. May our marriage reflect your grace and love as we endeavor to relate to each other in ways that glorify you.

(Record any insights and decisions in the Journal section.)

Devotional Date #2

Anyone who listens to my teaching and obeys me is wise, like a person who builds a house on solid rock. Though the rain comes in torrents and the floodwaters rise and the winds beat against that house, it won't collapse, because it is built on rock. But anyone who hears my teaching and ignores it is foolish, like a person who builds a house on sand. When the rains and floods come and the winds beat against that house, it will fall with a mighty crash.

Matthew 7:24-27 (NLT)

. . . .

A marriage based on ever-changing emotions and ideas is similar to a house built on shifting sand. It's foolish and leads to short-term solutions. Wise couples build their marriages on the unchanging, rock-solid foundation of God's Word. Jesus says the wise person not only hears his word, but also obeys it. The foolish person is the one who ignores what God says about marital behavior.

Jesus' story about the wise and foolish builders reminds me of two lighthouses built on the eastern shore of the United States. On the rocky coast of Maine, the Nubble Light stands upon a massive rock jutting out into the Atlantic Ocean. For more than 125 years, it has withstood the howling winds and surging waves of New England storms. It symbolizes the strength and endurance of building a marriage in such a way that it is strong from the very start. It is less costly, in many ways, to build on a solid foundation, using the right tools and materials. Couples whose marriages endure the waves that crash around and upon them will be a beacon of strength and hope for others.

Another lighthouse stands on the shifting sands of coastal North Carolina. The Cape Hatteras Lighthouse was built in 1870 on the barrier islands known as the Outer Banks. However, a little more than a hundred years later it was in peril because of the erosion of the beach by turbulent storms and tides. Originally built 1,600 feet from the sea, it was now only 160 feet from collapsing into the invading waves of the Atlantic Ocean. Concerned citizens launched a massive effort to save the lighthouse by relocating it a half-mile from its original site. The rescuers of the Cape Hatteras Lighthouse waited almost too long in their efforts to save it. Had it been built on a more solid foundation, a lot of money, time, and energy would have been saved.

The Bible, God's Word, is the spiritual foundation upon which to build a great marriage. As you read and listen to its wisdom, putting into practice what you learn, you will establish a rock solid spiritual foundation.

Let's Talk About It

1. How are you building a great spiritual foundation for your marriage? What changes need to be made?

2. In the past week, how did you apply a spiritual truth to the way you responded to a situation in your marriage?

3. How can your spouse pray for you in the coming week?

Prayer

Father, your Word is a light to our path in marriage. Guide us into all truth and teach us to obey your Word. Help us build our lives and marriage on a solid foundation so that we can stand complete in your will for us.

(Record any insights and decisions in the Journal section.)

Devotional Date #3

Though one may be overpowered, two can defend themselves. A cord of three strands is not quickly broken.

Ecclesiastes 4:12

. . . .

Faith in a personal God who loves you and is concerned for your well-being is fundamental to building a great marriage. I'm not talking about accepting a certain creed or belonging to a religious organization. I am talking about an intimate, personal relationship with God, made possible by confessing your sinfulness and inviting Jesus Christ to be your personal Savior and the master of your life and marriage.

Your marriage is deeply enriched when you are living in a vital relationship with God and endeavoring to express that relationship in practical terms. You bring to your marriage a perspective quite different from the popular "what's in it for me" culture. Marriage counselors agree that the biggest obstacle to overcoming marital troubles is selfishness. When my way is more important than my marriage, a crack develops in the marital foundation.

A vital relationship with God and a deliberate determination to live out biblical principles counteracts our instinctive tendency towards selfishness. Servanthood, sacrifice, trust, and esteeming others better than ourselves are key relational teachings of the Bible.

Your relationship with God also tempers the potentially rash decisions and verbal explosions that threaten great marriages. It keeps you from getting into trouble and provides a way out. The presence of God's Spirit in your marriage is a powerful resource. It helps you confess your wrongs to each other and grant forgiveness as required.

God-centered spouses are more satisfied in their marriages. They

● ● ●

consistently rate their marriages as stronger and more satisfying spiritually, emotionally, socially, and sexually. The source of that strength
is seen in this verse, "Though one may be overpowered, two can defend themselves. A cord of three strands is not quickly broken"
(Ecclesiastes 4:12). You, your spouse, and God form an unbreakable
cord.

Let's Talk About It

1. In what ways is your marriage uniquely Christian?

2. What does it mean to be a "God-centered spouse?"

3. How can your spouse pray for you in the coming week?

Prayer

*Heavenly Father, draw us closer to you with gentle cords of love and grace.
Show us how our marriage can glorify you. Create within us hearts to seek and
serve you all the days of our lives.*

(Record any insights and decisions in the Journal section.)

Devotional Date #4

I pray that out of his glorious riches he may strengthen you with power through his Spirit in your inner being, so that Christ may dwell in your hearts through faith. And I pray that you, being rooted and established in love, may have power, together with all the saints, to grasp how wide and long and high and deep is the love of Christ, and to know this love that surpasses knowledge — that you may be filled to the measure of all the fullness of God.

Ephesians 3:16-19

. . . .

D o not underestimate the power of prayer in your marriage. It is by prayer that we enlist the influence of God in our lives. We ask him to do what we cannot do. When a couple prays, it has several effects.

It helps you with your perspective on problems, and clears your vision so you can see what God wants in the foggy, murky moments of your lives. Your heart is quieted. You cannot worry and pray at the same time. The Bible says, "Do not be anxious about anything, but in everything, by prayer and petition, with thanksgiving, present your requests to God. And the peace of God, which transcends all understanding, will guard your hearts and your minds in Christ Jesus" (Philippians 4:6-7). Through prayer, you can gain God's perspective on an issue, which helps you discover the solution to your dilemma.

Prayer helps you reorder your priorities. It activates your faith in God, puts him and his plan first in your lives, and forces you to leave the situation with him. Through prayer, you can also find that what you highly value may be a deterrent to God's blessings in your home.

Prayer gives you a sense of purpose. Through contact with God, you discover how he wants to use your marriage for his glory. Your prayers reduce your daily cares and keep you in a place where God can use you most effectively.

How do you make prayer a significant part of your marriage? First, agree together that you will make this a priority in your marriage. The biggest reason couples give for not praying is the lack of time. The truth is that we make time for what we want. Find a mutually agreeable time to pray together. You may have to get up a few minutes before the kids so you can have some privacy, or turn off the TV earlier in the evening so you can pray before you go to bed.

Keep the prayer time brief. It is not necessary to pray for hours as a couple in order to have a meaningful prayer life. If one of you is not comfortable praying aloud, the shorter time will be encouraging. You can always extend the time when that is mutually agreeable.

Let's Talk About It

1. How can or how does prayer influence your marriage relationship?

2. What can you do to improve the spiritual intimacy in your marriage?

3. How can your spouse pray for you now and in the coming week?

Prayer

We praise you, Lord!
We give thanks to you, for you are good;
For your love and mercy endures forever.

(Record any insights and decisions in the Journal section.)

Devotional Date # 5

I urge you to live a life worthy of the calling you have received. Be completely humble and gentle; be patient, bearing with one another in love.

Ephesians 4:1-2

. . . .

A house foundation appears strong on the outside, even if it does not have enough steel rebar reinforcing the concrete. However, the weight of the house and its contents, coupled with changes in the earth's surface, will reveal its weakness and its lack of authenticity.

Authenticity describes something that is trustworthy, true, and reliable. Consistency would be another way of saying it. An authentic person lives a life that matches his or her values and priorities.

A couple building an authentic marriage that glorifies God will not tolerate inconsistency between their core faith values (or beliefs) and their actions in marriage. For example, Cindy and I believe strongly that we should worship together with other believers. That means we do not debate whether we go to church. Of course, I was a local church pastor for many years, which meant I had to be there. However, even when we are on vacation we do not avoid gathering with other Christians to worship God and learn from the Bible. The practicing of this core spiritual value helps us bond as a couple and strengthens us for any stormy weather in our marriage.

Our commitment to an authentic Christian lifestyle influences many areas of our life together. Our TV and movie choices are guided by that commitment. So is how we spend our money, how we deal with behaviors that can be addictive, and the way we treat each other daily.

To know what is right and not do it, tears at the fibers of your integrity. It weakens the soul of your marriage. Remember, the spiritual character of your marriage is the result of how you live what you believe.

Let's Talk About It

1. How does your marriage match your values and priorities?

2. What changes would you make in your marriage to reflect an authentic Christian lifestyle?

3. How can your spouse pray for you now and in the coming week?

Prayer

Lord Jesus, we trust in you to create in our marriage a reflection of who you are. In all our ways, we acknowledge you and lean not on our own wisdom and understanding.

(Record any insights and decisions in the Journal section.)

Devotional Date #6

*A man will leave his father and mother and be united to his wife,
and they will become one flesh."*

Genesis 2:24

. . . .

Many people act as if marriage is simply a human invention, rather than an institution rooted in creation. In the beginning, God created us male and female to walk together, side by side, for a lifetime. In this sacred design, the love of a man and a woman is made complete in the wholeness of their life together in the covenant of marriage.

Marriage, as designed by God, begins with a leaving of all other relationships. Perhaps you have heard that the wedding ring is designed to cut off your circulation. It's not that you and your spouse spend the rest of your lives in solitary confinement. Rather, the bonds to others must be altered in character, so that the man's full commitment is now to his wife and the woman's full commitment is now to her husband. The effect of this principle is that other things and relationships are given a lesser priority – business, career, church activities, parents, friends, and even children. All these must be placed in proper perspective. Whatever is important to you in this life, aside from a relationship with God, should be less important than your marriage.

Another element in God's design for marriage is that a man and a woman "become one flesh." This is more than simple togetherness. It is the blending of two lives into one – one in mind, heart, body, and spirit. This unity and oneness in marriage is a lifelong process, not an instant fact. Being pronounced husband and wife at the altar makes you one in the legal sense of the word, but what you do in the rest of your married life determines the practical outcome of becoming one. It requires holy wisdom, understanding, and knowledge for completion. It is one man and one woman willingly blending into each other's lives and seeking to glorify God as they do.

Let's Talk About It

1. Are there any activities or relationships that have taken a priority over your marriage relationship (other than your relationship with God)? What can you do to correct the imbalance?

2. How can your spouse pray for you now and in the coming week?

Prayer

Father, you want our marriage to last a lifetime, filled with your love and grace. We ask you to protect, preserve, and sustain it. We do not want sin, the Devil, circumstances, difficulties, or other people to separate what you have joined together. Knit together our hearts in complete unity.

(Record any insights and decisions in the Journal section.)

Devotional Date #7

Whoever wants to become great among you must be your servant, and whoever wants to be first must be slave of all. For even the Son of Man did not come to be served, but to serve, and give his life as a ransom for many.

Mark 10:43-45

. . . .

As a little child, your parents took care of you and provided for your care and nurture. You didn't have to do much. As you got older, your parents gave you more responsibilities, but they were still responsible for providing you with the basic needs of food, shelter, clothing, and education. Moving into single adulthood, you learned to take care of yourself. Then, you were married and discovered you had to put someone else first. That can take some adjusting.

Cecil Osborne wrote in *Understanding Your Mate*, "There are many reasons for the breakup of marriages, but the most common one is never found in divorce complaints: both of the marriage partners are waiting for each other to meet their needs." A vital tool in building a great marriage is mutual servanthood, or becoming a host. It's one of the fundamental things that makes a marriage work and last for a lifetime.

When you are a guest, everything is done for you. You feel no sense of responsibility or initiative. It's nice to be a guest, to be entertained and pampered, just to relax, indulge, and enjoy. However, if each marriage partner is hoping to be a guest, expecting the other to exercise initiative for his or her benefit, there will be big trouble. Both will be disappointed. The marriage becomes stale, loses its attractiveness, and an affair becomes tempting.

In a great marriage, each spouse focuses on becoming a host, not a guest in the relationship. In so doing, we follow the example of Jesus as noted in the Bible passage for this Devotional Date. Servanthood is an essential and distinguishing feature of true greatness. Even Jesus did not consider servanthood beneath his calling. Jesus did not sit around waiting for his disciples to serve him. His mission and life on earth focused on others as he fed the multitudes, healed the sick, and raised the dead. In addition, he came to earth to meet our greatest need – salvation from the consequences of sin.

No marriage can accommodate selfish people who think only about themselves. Selfishness drives people apart, leaving no room for compromise and teamwork.

Let's Talk About It

1. What do you think would be the greatest improvement in your marriage if you and your spouse became better servants of one another?

2. What is the most significant change you would have to make to see this happen?

3. How can your spouse pray for you now and in the coming week?

Prayer

Lord Jesus, one of the greatest things you have shown us is the importance of serving one another – to see our spouse's needs and find loving ways to meet them. Fill our hearts with your love, grace, and mercy so that we can serve each other joyfully.

(Record any insights and decisions in the Journal section.)

Devotional Date #8

Do nothing from selfish ambition or vain conceit, but in humility consider others better than yourselves. Each of you should look not only to your own interests, but also to the interests of others.

Philippians 2:3-4

. . . .

I read about a wedding where the groom, instead of going through the traditional garter ceremony, brought out a basin of water and washed his bride's feet. The wedding guests probably thought he was crazy, but he had it right. Most people do not enter marriage thinking about becoming a servant.

Mutual service is a powerful tool in great marriages because God intended your union to be a partnership, with each of you equally responsible for the marriage's well-being. Becoming a host in your marriage means, without expecting something in return, you persistently watch for ways to love, assist, support, praise, appreciate, protect, and please your spouse.

A complaint heard often in a distressed marriage is, "My spouse doesn't respect me or my needs." Marriage can be demanding and frustrating. At times, you may find yourself not being courteous to each other. You stop seeing your spouse as important, and begin putting other things – work, hobbies or the children – before the marriage.

What happens to your spouse when you think only about what you want or need? It's as if you were standing on his or her air hose. Emerson Eggrichs, author of *Love and* Respect, says that just as we need air to breathe, we all have certain emotional needs we want met in marriage. If you step on your spouse's air hose for any length of time, cutting off the oxygen supply, you can expect him or her to start thrashing around to get that need met. Your spouse might even step on your air hose to see if you will get the message.

The same thing happens when needs are not met in marriage. A spouse, who longs for love, attention, respect, and acceptance, may lash out with negative attacks that create more distance in the marriage. On the other hand, they may take a passive-aggressive approach, "I won't meet any of your needs until you meet my needs."

God values a spirit of humility and servanthood, and expects us to display this attribute in our marriages. Desperate households are filled with competing egos. Households devoted to God work to cultivate a servant heart in their relationships. A marriage characterized by prideful attitudes is destined for trouble. Blaise Pascal, a 17th century philosopher and theologian, declared, "The virtue of a man ought to be measured, not by his extraordinary exertions, but by his everyday conduct." How true! The way you daily serve as a host in your marriage reveals the heart you have for your spouse.

Couples in great marriages make the needs of their spouse a priority and resist the urge to take each other for granted.

Let's Talk About It

1. What are three needs your spouse recently met? How did it make you feel?

2. Do you need to apologize for any selfishness you displayed in the past week?

3. How can your spouse pray for you now and in the coming week?

Prayer

Heavenly Father, we agree not to give ourselves over to a selfish desire that will cause division and distrust in our marriage. We ask you to help us to be kind, tenderhearted, compassionate, understanding and loving toward one another.

(Record any insights and decisions in the Journal section.)

Devotional Date #9

Be completely humble and gentle; Be patient, bearing with one another in love.
Make every effort to keep the unity of the spirit through the bond of peace.

Ephesians 4:2-3

. . . .

To think that you must meet every need of your spouse is foolish, exhausting, and impossible. However, four fundamental needs are basic to building a great marriage.

The Need for Attention – Each of us wants to be noticed for who we are and for what we do. Bad marriages always include self-centered people. It's all about them. Mature people, who think beyond themselves, build great marriages. Instead of seeing marriage as a place to get attention, mature people make it a place where attention is given generously. It's not what you want or how you are doing. It's more about a focus on your spouse.

The Need for Acceptance – A genuine desire to serve my wife encourages me to satisfy her need for acceptance. Accepting her unconditionally tells her I have an awareness of her unique value as my wife. Demanding that your spouse match your fantasies is an insult. It breeds division, resentment, and anger. Unconditional acceptance of your mate's individual value is so important. If you accept only in part, you can love only in part. Acceptance does not necessarily mean approval. It does mean accepting reality as it is. It recognizes what cannot be changed, as well as what can be changed. In a great marriage, acceptance is willing to live with the differences.

The Need for Affection – A host in a great marriage will also seek to meet his or her spouse's need for affection. The things that sparked the passion in the days of courtship and early marriage – touching, holding hands, hugging, and kissing – cannot be stashed away in the closet with all of the old wedding announcements. You don't build a great marriage with the attitude of the guy who asked, "Why do you have to keep chasing the bus once you've caught it?" Couples wanting to have a great marriage will work together to express affection in ways they each genuinely appreciate.

The Need for Admiration – Your spouse also has a need for admiration. Most people's emotional stability is enhanced or diminished by what others think and say about them. Some of us go months and even years without giving a personal word of admiration to our spouse, and wonder why the relationship seems to be in a rut. When you affirm your spouse with loving words and deeds, your spouse is more likely to love you deeper. To build a great marriage on a daily basis, actively look for the positive. Concentrate on your spouse's strengths. You already know the weak areas, so look for strengths. Give honest compliments. Fight the urge to point out his or her short-comings and focus on what you appreciate about your spouse.

Let's Talk About It

1. Discuss with your spouse some of the ways in which he or she is meeting or could meet the needs in your life listed above.

2. How can your spouse pray for you now and in the coming week?

Prayer

Heavenly Father, make us sensitive to each other's needs and enable us to serve one another in those vital areas. Heal us of any hurts that threaten to create division in our marriage.

(Record any insights and decisions in the Journal section.)

Devotional Date #10

Love never gives up, never loses faith, is always hopeful, and endures through every circumstance.

1 Corinthians 13:4-7 (NLT)

. . . .

Eventually, every good marriage hits a rough patch. In your marriage vows, you promised to love regardless of all the changes and adversities, regardless of the good times or the bad times, and regardless of whether you live in wealth or poverty. I heard someone comment that instead of going into a marriage vowing, "till death do us part," maybe brides and grooms should be asked, "Do you have any idea how difficult this is going to be?"

A great marriage embodies a love of commitment, endurance, and perseverance. Not particularly romantic, is it? However, a relationship solely based on romance and emotions has an average life span of about two years. You have to have something more to make it last a lifetime.

The something more is an *enduring love*, which is the ability to stick with the relationship through the changing seasons of life. The Apostle Paul described this enduring love in the famous "love chapter" of the Bible:

> *Love is patient and kind. Love is not jealous or boastful or proud or rude. Love does not demand its own way. Love is not irritable, and it keeps no record of when it has been wronged. It is never glad about injustice but rejoices whenever the truth wins out. Love never gives up, never loses faith, is always hopeful, and endures through every circumstance. – 1 Corinthians 13:4-7(NLT)*

When you look closely at these verses, you can learn several things about this holy kind of love:

- *It is an active love – something you do.* You are patient when his dirty clothes continually miss the clothes hamper. You are kind when she borrows your tools, but forgets to put them back in the toolbox.

- *It is premeditated.* You decide ahead of time to respond in a loving manner when you are proven wrong in the middle of an intense argument.

- *It is observable.* You can see it in action. It's not just an emotion that is deep within your soul, only known to you. Other people see whether you are rude to each other, whether you are selfish and demanding, and whether you hold grudges.

- *It is measurable and verifiable.* You can quantify it. Elizabeth Barrett Browning wrote, "How do I love thee? Let me count the ways." Her answer was a list of the ways she measured that love – the depth, the height, and the breadth of it.

Let's Talk About It

1. Compare and contrast what people usually mean by the word *love* with how the Bible defines it.

2. Describe to your spouse how he or she recently practiced two of the characteristics of love listed in 1 Corinthians 13:4-7.

3. How can your spouse pray for you now and in the coming week?

Prayer

Heavenly Father, deliver us from jealousy, pride, rudeness, and thoughtlessness. Grant us a love that always protects, always trusts, always hopes, and always perseveres.

(Record any insights and decisions in the Journal section.)

• • •

Devotional Date #11

Be very careful, then, how you live—not as unwise but as wise, making the most of every opportunity, because the days are evil.

Ephesians 5:15-16

. . . .

George and Melissa remembered two significant moments in their marriage. The first happened when they looked at each other near the beginning of their relationship with the full knowledge of loving and being loved. They felt fully alive. Fifteen years later, they stood before each other and suddenly saw a stranger. Their relationship and attitudes had been shaped by too many hurts and unresolved anger. Fighting had become the norm rather than the exception in their marriage. Emotionally drained from all of the struggles, they were considering a trial separation. No longer was their love fully alive.

Was there anything George and Melissa could have done to avoid their situation? Are there practical steps you can take to avoid landing in the same place? If you are where they were, can you rekindle the flame that once burned between you? My answer is a resounding, "Yes!" There are three things you can do to keep love alive in your marriage.

Do Not Forget to be Married. Couples let many things intrude on their marriage relationship – careers, hobbies, friends, and even children. So much energy is put into these other roles, there is little left for their relationship. To keep love alive in your marriage, you must give top priority to maintaining a loving relationship with your spouse. If your work or even your children have become the primary focus of your life, you need to refocus on your spouse, rather than looking to another individual or group of people to meet your emotional needs.

Put each area of your life into proper perspective.

Cherish and Respect Your Spouse as Your Best Friend. The core of marriage is a friendship built on emotional closeness, acceptance of one another, and a fulfilling companionship. In survey after survey, the overwhelming majority of couples in successful long-term marriages reported that they had become best friends. Best friends practice several key habits. They stay in touch with each other as they share themselves and their experiences, support each other during troubled times, and consistently affirm one another. They also have discovered the tremendous value of mutually respecting each other.

Develop Rituals for Fun. Keeping love alive in a great marriage does not mean you must focus exclusively on problems nor have an emotionally deep and intimate discussion. Spending time having fun together, on a regular basis, is a powerful deterrent to a stale marriage. As married life becomes busier, humor often fades, and no time remains for fun. Stressed and tired, couples feel overwhelmed with responsibilities. Fun is a powerful tool in relieving stress. Make sure you plan regular time alone as a couple for fun.

Let's Talk About It

1. What are the obstacles to your having fun? What can you do to overcome them?

2. In the early years (or days) of your marriage, what did you do for fun? Pick one of them to repeat this week or in the near future.

3. How can your spouse pray for you now and in the coming week?

Prayer

Heavenly Father, thank you for our marriage. Help us to make it a priority in our daily lives so that our love will remain alive and joyful.

(Record any insights and decisions in the Journal section.)

• • •

Devotional Date #12

And now these three remain: faith, hope and love.
But the greatest of these is love.

1 Corinthians 13:13

. . . .

To succeed in marriage you must be able to adjust to each other's unique personalities and opinions. I remember reading about two porcupines in Alaska that kept warm by cuddling together. Because their quills pricked each other, they moved apart. Soon they were shivering again, and had to cuddle for their own survival. They needed each other, even though they *needled* each other! The only way they were able to survive was by continually adjusting their quills.

Adjusting to each other does not mean you have to understand your spouse fully. I will never understand how Cindy, my wife, can adoringly hold a mouse in her hands, but let out the most horrific scream when she sees a spider on the other side of the room. She will never understand why I don't enjoy swimming as much as she does.

A spouse's willingness to adjust comes from a heart that is grateful for the strengths that exist, rather than frustrated by what is missing. It can be difficult at times to accept your spouse with all of his or her unique and individual traits. When you think about it, those are probably the very attributes that first attracted you to each other. Making adjustments in your attitude about your spouse will result in respect and thanksgiving.

Adjusting to meet your spouse's needs does not mean that you try to become a different person. You are simply adjusting your behavior to meet your spouse's needs in order to build a mutually satisfying relationship. For example, you leave the bedroom window up when you would rather have it down.

As you better understand your spouse and honestly appreciate his or her uniqueness, are you willing and able to adjust your relating style to meet your mate's needs? The critical issue in building a great marriage relationship is not the compatibility of your personalities or behavioral styles. Rather, it is the commitment to understanding and adjusting to the one your heart loves.

Let's Talk About It

1. What were the unique traits and features that attracted you to your spouse?

2. God loves us in spite of our flaws. How does marriage teach you to love your spouse in spite of the things that you think are annoying?

3. How can your spouse pray for you now and in the coming week?

Prayer

Heavenly Father, only you are perfect. Forgive us when we have failed to appreciate each other's unique qualities. You established our marriage and gave us each other, specially designed by you. Help us to adjust our responses in order to love like you.

(Record any insights and decisions in the Journal section.)

Devotional Date #13

Therefore, as God's chosen people, holy and dearly loved, clothe yourselves with compassion, kindness, humility, gentleness and patience. Bear with each other and forgive one another if any of you has a grievance against someone. Forgive as the Lord forgave you. And over all these virtues put on love, which binds them all together in perfect unity.

Colossians 3:12-14

. . . .

We are different in the way we look, think, relate, talk, act, and approach life. That's not by accident. It's all a part of God's original design. Harold L. Myra wrote about this diversity of God's creation, including humans:

God's creation is remarkably diverse: from penguins to horses to Persian cats. Each feeds, mates, seeks shelter, but their sharp differences make for a fascinating world. People, too, are diverse. The principles for marriage may be the same for each couple: commitment, communication, shared values. But as we emphasize the commonalities, let's equally celebrate every couple as unique.[1]

Countless words have been written about the way in which men and women are different. Bill and Pam Ferrel say that men are like waffles. They are not saying that men waffle on decisions and are generally unstable. Instead, men approach life in what social scientists call compartmentalizing – putting life and responsibilities into different compartments, like the sections of a waffle. Men tend to have room for only one issue in each box. When your husband is at work, he is in the at-work-box. When he is watching TV, he is in his TV box.

---

[1] Harold L. Myra, *Conan or Cosby*, Marriage Partnership (Spring 1988), 48.

In contrast, women process life more like a plate of pasta. On a plate of spaghetti, there are many individual noodles that all touch one another. The Ferrels point out that if you follow one noodle around the plate, it will intersect with other noodles, and you might even end up following another noodle.

For my wife, it seems that every issue and thought is linked to every other issue and thought in some way. I sometimes get whiplash trying to keep up with her in our conversations. I respond to something she says and find out she has already moved on to another topic. What did I miss? When did she change topics? I am a professionally trained listener. I teach other people how to listen. This does not bode well for me. Once I asked her to give me a signal that she had moved on to another topic. She just gave me the "look." You know what I mean?

Let's Talk About It

1. How are your marital interactions impacted by your unique ways of processing life either positively or negatively?

2. How can you use your differences to strengthen your marriage?

3. How can your spouse pray for you now and in the coming week?

Prayer

Heavenly Father, true love comes from you! Understanding how you graciously love us definitely helps us love each other sacrificially and wholeheartedly. May your love characterize our individual lives as we build our marriage relationship.

(Record any insights and decisions in the Journal section.)

Devotional Date #14

Since we live by the Spirit, let us keep in step with the Spirit. Let us not become conceited, provoking and envying each other.

Galatians 5:25-26

. . . .

Ignoring or suppressing the positive value of our differences will only heighten conflict and dissatisfaction in the marriage. People wrestle desperately to relate freely and openly. Because of the sinful nature we inherited, marriage can become a frustrating struggle – a mixture of selfishness, dissatisfaction, embarrassment, and resentment. Differences will not destroy your marriage. Instead, the *way* in which you handle these differences has a greater influence on the outcome of your marriage.

By failing to be aware of each other's strengths and differences, we are in danger of ignoring each other's needs. Moreover, when we ignore those needs, we inflict wounds of misunderstanding, and love is not conveyed.

Misunderstandings are the result of two people seeing things differently. Your spouse may have different needs, values, life perspectives, goals, and fears. In many cases, the differences that initially brought you together may be the differences that will push you away from each other.

Gaining an understanding of how you and your spouse are different is a great tool for making a relationship work. Realizing that your spouse's actions result from his or her unique style of relating, rather than being a tactic designed to anger or offend you, changes how you view his or her behavior. It is no longer interpreted as a threat or an affront to you.

This new level of understanding leads to a loving and kind relationship. What is certain is that if your spouse does not feel understood, he or she will not feel accepted and loved. On the other hand, when your spouse feels loved, he or she also feels accepted and understood.

Consider what is happening in this couple's relationship. The husband enjoys long moments of quietness and time alone for thinking and meditating. His wife, however, is just the opposite. She continually has a project going and loves to cross things off her *To Do* list. When she begins to feel overwhelmed at the amount of things that she has said "yes" to, she approaches her husband for help. "Since you're not doing anything," she interrupts, "come and help me hang these pictures." Not doing anything? He is offended at that comment. How do you think he feels?

Taking the time to understand what you each value and need in your marriage is a tool that leads to love and acceptance.

Let's Talk About It

1. Have you ever had an intense argument with your spouse and walked away wondering what it was all about? What were the results? How could it have been handled in a more positive way?

2. What are two things you value or need that would strengthen your marriage?

3. How can your spouse pray for you now and in the coming week?

Prayer

Heavenly Father, a marriage that is under your influence will produce a great harvest of love, understanding, and acceptance. We invite you to bring the full influence of the Holy Spirit into our hearts, our minds, our actions, and our marriage.

(Record any insights and decisions in the Journal section.)

Devotional Date #15

So speak encouraging words to one another. Build up hope so you'll all be together in this, no one left out, no one left behind. I know you're already doing this; just keep on doing it.

1 Thessalonians 5:11 (THE MESSAGE)

· ·

The cartoon box opens with Lucy and Linus in their living room. Linus, curled up in a chair, quietly reads a book. Lucy, standing behind him, has a funny look on her face. She turns to Linus and says, "It's very strange. It happens just by looking at you."

"What happens?" replies Linus.

Lucy calmly answers, "I can feel a criticism coming on."

Criticism and discouragement come as naturally as flying does to a goose. Our self-centered bent makes it much easier to criticize than to encourage. Verbal abuse is prevalent in many relationships, which can be as damaging as or more damaging than physical abuse. The emotional scars caused by constant criticism resist healing. This is not to minimize the tragic epidemic of physical abuse, but to underscore the scourge of emotional abuse in relationships.

When you fail to encourage your spouse, or when you replace encouragement with harsh criticism, you chip away at the foundation of your marriage. A large dose of encouragement is the solution.

According to the Bible, an encourager is one who is by someone's side, participating actively in the relationship rather than standing on the sidelines. An encourager is not pulling someone along, nor pushing from behind like a bulldozer. Instead, he or she comes alongside to help as a partner – not telling what needs to be done, but helping to do it.

Another valuable role of an encourager is to bring comfort and consolation in times of distress. We are to be at each other's side instead of at each other's throats. In times of distress, an encourager offers the stability needed to stand against the floods of adversity.

Have you seen geese flying along in a "V" formation? Scientists have noted that as each bird flaps its wings, it creates uplift for the bird immediately following. By flying in a V formation, the whole flock adds at least 71% greater flying range than if each bird flew on its own. When a goose falls out of formation, it suddenly feels the drag and resistance of trying to go it alone. It quickly gets into the formation to take advantage of the lifting power of the bird immediately in front. When the lead goose gets tired, he rotates back in the group and another goose moves up to the lead. The geese honk from behind to encourage those up front to keep up their speed. An encouraging word goes a long way.

It seems that if we have the sense of a goose, we will not miss opportunities to be an encourager in marriage.

Let's Talk About It

1. How does your spouse actively encourage you? How does it make you feel?

2. How is your marriage either like or unlike a flock of geese?

3. How can your spouse pray for you now and in the coming week?

Prayer

Heavenly Father, thank you for being our Great Encourager. Give us the sense of a goose in our marriage!

(Record any insights and decisions in the Journal section.)

Devotional Date #16

For the grace of God that brings salvation has appeared to all men. It teaches us to say "No" to ungodliness and worldly passions, and to live self-controlled, upright and godly lives in this present age, while we wait for the blessed hope – the glorious appearing of our great God and Savior, Jesus Christ, who gave himself for us to redeem us from all wickedness and to purify for himself a people that are his very own, eager to do what is good.

Titus 2:11-14

. . . .

No area of our lives could more urgently use a daily infusion of grace than our marriages. As you cultivate an appreciation for God's grace and apply that grace in your daily interactions, you position yourselves to experience a joy that only God can give.

The Apostle Paul's counsel to Titus (above) shows that sacred grace is constantly working in us, not just for salvation, but also for helping us grow in how we love and live. This sacred grace teaches us how to live in the unique, moment-by-moment days of our lives. It is always there like the coach or teacher who will not quit. What does it teach?

Grace teaches us to *renounce*; to turn from what is wrong – "ungodliness and worldly passions." The biggest challenge in our marriages is to resist the pull of the old selfish, sinful nature that still plagues our souls. Sacred grace meets us at these very crucial points of marriage with a desire to please God and with the power to overcome. For example, when your spouse hurls angry insults at you, or is disrespectful, or does something dumb, grace is there to help you renounce the phrases forming in your mind and the urge to punish that is erupting within your heart.

Living in a wise and mature way in your marriage comes not just from knowing what to avoid, but what to pursue. This sacred grace not only teaches us what to renounce, but also teaches us what to *embrace*; to turn toward what is right – "to live self-controlled, upright and godly lives." God's sanctifying grace helps us replace old patterns of behavior with godliness. In this daily presence and power of sacred grace, we find hope for a marriage that is fulfilling and lasting. It helps replace the less-than-godly passions of our hearts with kindness towards one another, patience with challenging moments, right thinking about each other, self-control of our tongues and anger, and a host of other motivations and actions that make our marriages sweet and safe.

Living with a spouse who stumbles in many ways just as you do, can exhaust every ounce of patience and understanding you have. Moods fluctuate, tempers flare, patience runs short and guilt often sets in. We need this sacred relational grace for those moments.

Let's Talk About It

1. How does your spouse mirror God's grace in your marriage?

2. What do you find appealing about the teaching aspect of sacred grace in a marriage relationship?

3. How can your spouse pray for you now and in the coming week?

Prayer

Father, we thank you for the abiding and enduring presence of your grace in our marriage. Through it, our marriage has been enriched in every way. Forgive us when we have withheld it from each other. May the grace of the Lord Jesus Christ reign in our lives and home.

(Record any insights and decisions in the Journal section.)

Devotional Date #17

*Catch for us the foxes, the little foxes that ruin the vineyards,
our vineyards that are in bloom.*

Song of Songs 2:15

. . . .

When couples lack the positive tools and skills for great communication, there is more *bad talk* than *love talk* in their daily lives. The importance of dealing with this bad talk is evident in the verse from the Song of Songs (above) as the wife urges her husband to capture the foxes that are ruining the vineyards.

Foxes are sly and stealthy, often portrayed as sneaking in to steal things, such as eggs in a henhouse. In the context of a vineyard, the foxes, if given free access, will get to the ripening grapes and ruin the harvest.

In marital communication, bad talk is like the "little foxes." If you do not control the bad talk, it can erase the good effects of just about everything else you have going for you.

Consider this brief listing of some of the "little foxes" that become negative communication tools:

- *Blame* – You say it is your spouse's fault and there is nothing wrong with you or with what you did.

- *Escalation* – You say or do something negative, and your spouse responds negatively. You respond to their criticism by criticizing them.

- *Painful Put-Downs* – You subtly or directly put down the thoughts, feelings, actions, or worth of your spouse.

- *Passive Aggression* – You pout, withdraw, or say nothing to get even with your spouse.

- *Hostile, Sarcastic Humor* – Your words and tone of voice communicate that you are not dealing with your conflict in an open and honest fashion.

- *Negative Interpretations* – You interpret your spouse's words or behavior more negatively than they intended.

- *Assumptions* – You assume you know how your spouse thinks or feels without checking it out.

- *Denial* – You insist that you don't feel angry, hurt, or sad when you really do.

- *Absolutes* – You use words like "never" and "always."

These negative communication tools are obvious indicators of whether you are going to have love talk or bad talk. You are doomed for failure when a conversation leads off with one of them. You might as well call a time out and start over.

Let's Talk About It

1. Which of the negative communication tools listed above are prevalent in your marital communication?

2. What can you do to protect your marriage from "the foxes?"

3. How can your spouse pray for you now and in the coming week?

Prayer

Father, help us speak the truth in love by honestly and openly sharing our thoughts and feelings without destroying each other. Let your grace continue to shape our hearts and our words.

(Record any insights and decisions in the Journal section.)

Devotional Date #18

My dove in the clefts of the rock, in the hiding places on the mountainside,
show me your face, let me hear your voice;
for your voice is sweet, and your face is lovely.

Song of Songs 2:14

. . . .

A desire to communicate is lacking in many marriages. Notice what the husband says in the verse above, "show me your face, let me hear your voice." He wanted her to come out from wherever she was and talk to him. He found her voice pleasing. He had a desire for communication. A desire to communicate will result in making time to talk.

One of the "little foxes" in so many marriages today is busyness. It is the nemesis of every marriage and it corrupts your conversations. So much of our talk takes place on the run – off to work or school or kid's games or whatever. Our *busy talk* tricks us into thinking that we are having meaningful conversations, when all we are trying to do is to make it to the end of the day.

Okay, you have a desire to have more than a few minutes of meaningful talk during your day, but how do you do it? The obvious answer is to slow down. Benjamin Franklin said, "Lost time is never found again." Therefore, you need to focus on the present moment. It's not all about the next appointment or task. What is happening in the present moment that you do not want to miss?

The seemingly routine moments of your day can be more meaningful when you have a desire to communicate with your spouse. For instance, what is it like when you come home at the end of the day? Do you greet each other with warm words or with complaints? Did you know that the first four minutes you are together sets the tone for the rest of the evening? It's true! A loving greeting, a tender kiss, or a lingering embrace will help set the environment for love talk. One busy husband found it helpful to use his long commute home to talk to his wife on his cell phone (using the hands-free attachment, of course). They discussed the day's events and prepared to reconnect at home. It turned their previously frustrating re-entry time into a more pleasant experience.

Do you find it hard to get excited about telling your spouse about your day? John Maxwell changed his conversations with his wife at the end of the day when he realized all she was getting were leftovers. During the day, he shared all the exciting things with his colleagues and friends. He had little enthusiasm for sharing it with his wife by the time he got home. Consequently, he started keeping things to himself until he could share them with her first.

You might be eating leftovers, but you can make the conversation fresh and encouraging.

Let's Talk About It

1. What challenges do you face as a couple that keep you from having meaningful conversations? How can you overcome them?

2. What are three things that happened to you today (or this week) and how did they make you feel?

3. How can your spouse pray for you now and in the coming week?

Prayer

Heavenly Father, we thank you for your love and grace freely given to us. You created us in your image and blessed our union with your Divine Presence. Help us to use our words and conversations as a help and support to one another.

(Record any insights and decisions in the Journal section.)

Devotional Date #19

My dove in the clefts of the rock, in the hiding places on the mountainside,
show me your face, let me hear your voice;
for your voice is sweet, and your face is lovely.

Song of Songs 2:14

. . . .

The request by the husband in Song of Songs, "Show me your face," signifies the desire for face-to-face communication. There is no hiding behind closed doors or speaking through walls. I'm not saying you can't have short bursts of conversation when in separate rooms, but you had better be sure you really heard what the other one said, or you're in big trouble.

Face-to-face conversations are better because you are able to give your attention to the verbal and non-verbal facets of the conversation. Natural eye contact, not staring or gazing off into who-knows-where, helps you communicate that you value your spouse's words. Paying attention to your spouse's body language helps you process the words you hear. It also helps your spouse make the right point. To illustrate this, look at how you can interpret the following non-verbal cues:

- Clenched Hands = anger, tension

- Crossed Arms = defensiveness, distance

- Hands on Hips = impatience

- Rubbing Neck = frustration, anger

Everything you do with your body is communicating a message whether you mean it or not. Telling your spouse, "I love you," with your hands firmly planted on your hips sends the wrong message.

For the important talks in your marriage, find a quiet place that makes it easier to pay attention to each other, and promotes good talk rather than bad talk. If your spouse is preoccupied, don't assume that he or she is ready to listen just because you are ready to talk.

Cindy and I had to work on this when I was watching mystery shows on television. It frustrated me – no, it made me angry – when she asked me an irrelevant question during the last few minutes, which usually resolved the mystery. It was not always a simple *yes* or *no* question, but one that required thought and an extended conversation. The result was that I missed the resolution of the mystery. As far as I was concerned, I had just wasted an hour of my life.

My wife should not have to take second place to a television show or movie, but I wanted to find out how the mystery was solved. We finally found a better way to do this. She asks if this is a good time to interrupt. If not, I let her know when.

A key to great communication is making sure you have each other's focused attention when it counts.

Let's Talk About It

1. Describe the influence, either positive or negative, of the non-verbal cues in your marital communication.

2. What practical things would help you have each other's focused attention when it counts?

3. How can your spouse pray for you now and in the coming week?

Prayer

Father, we ask that you help us grow in the area of communication so that we can talk to each other kindly and respond in love to each other. May your words be on our lips daily.

(Record any insights and decisions in the Journal section.)

● ● ●

Devotional Date #20

My dove in the clefts of the rock, in the hiding places on the mountainside,
show me your face, let me hear your voice;
for your voice is sweet, and your face is lovely.

Song of Songs 2:14

. . . .

In the verse from Song of Songs, the husband wants to hear his wife speak. He says, "let me hear your voice; for your voice is sweet." Words are powerful when used in the context of relationships.

Your words can bring blessing or cursing into your spouse's life. They can be life or death to him or her as noted in this verse, "The tongue has the power of life and death" (Proverbs 18:21). Words can help build an intimate relationship, but they can also destroy the very foundations of your marriage. Using words of blessing on a regular basis will protect your relationship from the negative emotions that sabotage a great marriage.

You may not feel like using positive words due to a conflict in your marriage. The last thing you want to do is *bless* your spouse; however, you have to start knocking down the walls that separate you. By using positive words, you can be the first to turn your conversations in a more encouraging direction. Your spouse may surprise you by responding in the same way.

You can bless your spouse with *words of acceptance.* We can communicate a lack of acceptance with careless words. I read about a husband on his honeymoon who told his new bride she had some weaknesses. Before he could list them, she responded, "Those weaknesses kept me from getting a better husband." What a way to start a marriage!

Using *words of affection* is another way to bless your spouse. I identify with the frightened little girl awakened in the middle of the night by thunder and lightning. As her father held her, he told her she did not need to worry because God loved her and would protect her. "I know God loves me," she said, "but right now I want someone with skin on to love me." We communicate that kind of love through our words.

A third positive way of talking is to use *words of affirmation*. Most of us are quick to criticize, but slow to praise. This is particularly true with those who are closest to us. Your spouse grows faster in the direction of your praise, than in the path of your criticism.

We need to be wise in how we choose and use our words. To control your tongue is not easy. However, with the help of the Holy Spirit for teaching and guidance, you have a better chance at success. An ancient proverb says it best, "It is wonderful to say the right thing at the right time!" (Proverbs 15:23, NLT).

Let's Talk About It

1. What kinds of statements discourage you? What kinds encourage you?

2. Do you need to apologize for any hurtful words you've used?

3. How can your spouse pray for you now and in the coming week?

Prayer

Father, help us to have open and honest communication in our marriage, encouraging vulnerability and authenticity. May we never be guilty of breaking each other's spirit. Instead, may we affirm and strengthen one another so that together we can endure any weakness or failure and not lose hope.

(Record any insights and decisions in the Journal section.)

Devotional Date #21

My dove in the clefts of the rock, in the hiding places on the mountainside,
show me your face, let me hear your voice;
for your voice is sweet, and your face is lovely.

Song of Songs 2:14

. . . .

The husband in Song of Songs invites his wife into a conversation where he wants to hear what she has to say. *Attentive listening* is probably the most important and the most difficult communication tool in our marital tool bags.

Courses on the art of speaking are readily available, but the art of listening is taken for granted. People complain about their spouse's failure to express opinions and feelings, but the more frequent complaint is about a spouse who is not listening.

The Bible speaks about the importance of being a ready listener, giving our focused attention to the one who is speaking. "My dear brothers, take note of this: Everyone should be quick to listen, slow to speak and slow to become angry" (James 1:19).

A wireless phone company immortalized these words, "Can you hear me now?" When we say that in marriage, we mean more than, "Do you hear my words?" We want to know, "Do you understand what I mean by what I say?" It's not enough to just hear the words. Do I understand the meaning of the words? I may hear my wife's words, but if I fail to understand the meaning behind those words, I miss the essential transmission and reception of feelings, attitudes, facts, and beliefs that occur in great marriages.

Some of us get into trouble when we pretend to listen. This listening style fakes interest, and communicates to your spouse that what he or she has to say is not important. If what I have to say is irrelevant, then I must be unimportant. The way you listen and respond to your spouse has an effect on his or her sense of value, which can either build a fulfilling relationship or put distance between you.

Being misunderstood is another key problem in marital communication. Couples in great marriages learn to slow down their conversations when things start to escalate in the wrong direction. They paraphrase what they heard and then ask, "Have I understood your message and motive?" When you listen attentively, without interruption, and paraphrase what you heard, your spouse knows whether his or her intended message was clearly understood. It also keeps you from responding to the wrong message. Remember, be quick to listen and slow to speak.

One more thing about listening, you cannot listen well unless you close your mouth and focus on what your spouse is saying. This attentive style of listening means that when my spouse is talking, I will not be thinking about what I am going to say when she stops talking. The wisdom of the Bible emphasizes this point, "Answering before listening is both stupid and rude" (Proverbs 18:13, THE MESSAGE).

Let's Talk About It

1. What are some good reasons for listening well in your marriage?

2. What are some things that make it difficult for you to listen well? What techniques would help you listen better?

3. How can your spouse pray for you now and in the coming week?

Prayer

Father, teach us to respond to what is said so that our mate knows he or she is being heard. Help us to keep a confidence, to build a wall of trust so that we are free to share all that is in our hearts. And as we listen, Lord, help us to avoid giving quick or pat answers. Help us to listen patiently.

(Record any insights and decisions in the Journal section.)

Devotional Date #22

Those who love money will never have enough. How absurd to think that wealth brings true happiness!

Ecclesiastes 5:10 (NLT)

. . . .

Overspending is a common obstacle to a great marriage. Too much debt creates a strain on the family checking account. It also causes couples to spend too much time working and worrying. With the average household in America carrying a credit card debt of $15,000, both spouses are forced to work, or one spouse takes on an extra job. The result is a lack of time and energy to build healthy relationships with each other and with their children.

Couples have trouble dealing with financial matters for a number of reasons. One spouse thinks the other one spends too much money. They disagree on how much to save and on priorities for purchases. Who controls the money is also a major battleground for a large percentage of couples.

While all couples argue about money, some arguments reveal more about the couple's ability to build a healthy relationship. Such arguments can mask larger concerns such as conflict over power and control in the marriage, differing values related to money, and a host of feelings that are associated with money for each spouse.

In the early days of our marriage, money was very tight. I was the youth pastor for a local church and Cindy was finishing her college degree. My job was our lone source of income. The only financial plan we had was to live within our means. I remember a time when I did not have any money in my wallet. That was not a good feeling. When invited to have lunch with a friend, I had to decline because I had no money in my wallet. When I approached Cindy to release some funds from our checking account, she saw no need for me to have this extra money. After all, she was not spending money needlessly. A full-fledged war of words followed.

We did not resolve this ongoing fight until we learned that having some money in my wallet was more about independence and security than it was about buying a cup of coffee. I felt like the child having to ask the parent for money. It wasn't good for our marriage.

We resolved the problem by instituting an allowance from the family account for each of us to spend or save as we pleased. It has worked for more than 40 years. Open and honest communication about these hidden issues was the first step to reducing the stress caused by money in our marriage.

Good financial management is a strategic tool for building a great marriage. If you don't learn to manage your money, it will manage you. Couples in great marriages agree on how to handle money.

Let's Talk About It

1. What are your core values about money? In other words, what do you believe about the role of money in your marriage – how it is earned, saved, and spent?

2. How have your core values about money and possessions influenced your marriage relationship? What would you like to change?

3. How can your spouse pray for you now and in the coming week?

Prayer

Lord, we ask for wisdom and harmony in our financial life as we serve you. Forgive us when we have been selfish, when we've gone to extremes of spending or hoarding. Help us not to argue, but to learn better ways to communicate—to be honest and to seek to understand the other person's perspective even when we may not agree.

(Record any insights and decisions in the Journal section.)

Devotional Date #23

Keep your lives free from the love of money and be content with what you have, because God has said, "Never will I leave you; never will I forsake you."

Hebrews 13:5

. . . .

We live in a culture that tells us what we have is not adequate. It's called consumerism – the purchasing and consuming of goods and materials in excess of our basic needs.

You could argue that consumerism was present in the Garden of Eden with Adam & Eve. Think about it. They had all they needed provided by God – food, shelter, companionship, a co-worker, peace. However, they were not satisfied. They wanted more.

Sound familiar? Dissatisfaction with what they had and desiring to have it all led to their downfall – and ours. God teaches us to live by a different principle – the principle of contentment.

I saw a cartoon of a married couple standing next to a glistening new car in an auto dealer's showroom. The wife is busily punching the keypad of her handheld calculator. The irritated husband says, "Now, dear, you know we need a new car. Stop trying to figure out how many starving children we could feed if we drive the old clunker another year." This illustrates the dilemma in which I often find myself – a struggle between what I want and what I should do.

Confronted with the opportunity to purchase a truck, I sat down to see if we could afford it. I wanted it and I wanted it badly. Cindy did not agree. She is our bookkeeper and has her finger on the pulse of our family finances. Our current vehicles were fine, but I wanted a truck.

"Why do you want a truck?" she asked.

"So I can haul stuff," I declared.

After reviewing our financial picture numerous times, it was wretchedly apparent that I would be risking our financial strength to buy the truck. I did not buy the truck.

Rather than improving one's life, people who are more consumeristic tend to have lower satisfaction with their lives. They also have a greater tendency to spend compulsively, have higher incidences of depression, and lower ethical standards.

Solomon wrote, "Don't weary yourself trying to get rich. Why waste your time? For riches can disappear as though they had the wings of a bird!" (Proverbs 23:4-5, NLT) Why chase after something that can just fly away? True, lasting contentment is learned through trusting God for our daily needs and living within our means.

Contentment, rather than out of control consumption, is a better testimony of God's presence in our homes.

Let's Talk About It

1. Think of the things you have spent the most money on in recent years. Which purchases are you most content with? Which purchases bother you the most?

2. How content are you with what you have? If you are content, how do you handle the pressure to "keep up" or conform to a higher standard of living? If you're not very content, why do you think you feel that way?

3. How can your spouse pray for you now and in the coming week?

Prayer

Heavenly Father, we thank you for your provision in our life together. You always provide for us and fulfill our needs. May we be good stewards of all that you give us. May money never cause tension in our marriage or be a source of pain. We pray that contentment in you will reign in our hearts.

(Record any insights and decisions in the Journal section.)

Devotional Date #24

Get rid of all bitterness, rage and anger, brawling and slander, along with every form of malice. Be kind and compassionate to one another, forgiving each other, just as in Christ God forgave you.

Ephesians 4:31-32

. . . .

You do not have to be married very long before you start tripping over a few relational snags. There is conflict in the best of marriages. When I hear married couples say that they never have any conflicts, I assume one of several possibilities:

- They have not been married very long.
- They do not know each other very well.
- They do not talk to each other very much.
- They are lying!

Conflict is painful. It brings out anger, fear, and anxiety, all of the emotional experiences we try to avoid. However, not all conflict is bad. It can provide an opportunity for growth in a relationship. Like dynamite, it is helpful if used right, but destructive if used at the wrong time or in the wrong manner. Through healthy conflict, couples learn to appreciate, understand, and accept other points of view. They focus on how to manage conflict successfully when it does arise.

Conflict in marriage is unavoidable, but combat is optional. When hurt or offended by your spouse, you have at least three response options: get even, ignore the offense, or face the anger and hurt so you can resolve the conflict.

Revenge has never been a good option. It may be sweet for the moment, but the long-term result is not so pleasurable. Revenge is not a laughing matter. An angry spouse may withhold intimacy, affection, or kindness as a means of revenge. The desire to get even has led to bankruptcy, adultery, and abuse.

A second option in conflict is to ignore the offense or hurt. There may be times when this is appropriate. Your spouse is having a bad day and you know that he or she is not intentionally trying to hurt you. There are times when it may be wise to ignore a conflict because you don't know how to resolve it without creating an even bigger conflict.

However, denying your anger, holding it in, or never expressing it to your spouse, leads to resentment, hate, and revenge. The inevitable result is a violent explosion of words, and sometimes, physical abuse. All of your unresolved anger spews out without regard for how it wounds and pushes your spouse even farther from you. One of the most destructive things that can happen to a marriage is to have the growing sense that you are living in a minefield.

It doesn't have to be this way, or ever get to be this way in the first place. There is a third option for dealing with marital conflict. You can face the anger and hurt so that you can resolve the conflict in a healthy manner. Even in the moments of anger, betrayal, exasperation, and hurt, God wants you to pursue your spouse with the goal of reconciling and embracing him/her with his love in you.

Let's Talk About It

1. Give an example of how conflict has been either good or bad for your marriage.

2. What keeps you from dealing with conflict in a healthy manner?

3. How can your spouse pray for you now and in the coming week?

Prayer

Heavenly Father, we ask you to help us deal with conflict in our marriage in a healthy manner. Please guide us in how we respond to each other.

(Record any insights and decisions in the Journal section.)

Devotional Date #25

Since God chose you to be the holy people whom he loves, you must clothe your-selves with tenderhearted mercy, kindness, humility, gentleness, and patience. You must make allowance for each other's faults and forgive the person who offends you. Remember, the Lord forgave you, so you must forgive others. And the most important piece of clothing you must wear is love. Love is what binds us all to-gether in perfect harmony.

Colossians 3:12-14 (NLT)

. . . .

In the popular movie, *Home Alone*, eight-year-old Kevin found himself sitting in a church beside his elderly neighbor, a bedrag-gled old man who was the subject of frightening rumors among the neighborhood children. The man was there during his grand-daughter's Christmas choir rehearsal because he knew he would not be welcomed during the performance.

Years before, he and his son had a grievance that erupted into harsh words and flailing fists. The old man was not allowed to see his beautiful granddaughter, so he sneaked in when he would not be no-ticed. Sensing his anguish and pain, Kevin asked him this simple question: "Why don't you just go to your son and tell him you're sorry?" The old man mumbled that it was not that simple, and left.

Resolving marital feuds is neither simple, nor easy; however, one of the quickest ways to end a fight is to admit when you are wrong, and seek forgiveness. The goal is not to win an argument. The goal should always be to heal the relationship. To seek a solution that will result in a stronger marriage, greater understanding, and a deeper love often involves the giving and receiving of forgiveness.

A willingness to forgive heals hurts and helps spouses feel ac-cepted and connected. It offers a fresh start after you have offended and hurt each other. The absence of forgiveness pushes you apart. You may even use your spouse's sins to justify pulling away from him or her.

Love that is infused with forgiveness is a powerful tool in marriage. It frees you for a restored relationship with your spouse, because you choose not to hold it against her or to get even with him. Depending on the magnitude of the offense, you may not be able to eradicate it from your memory, but you can choose not to dwell on it. Focusing on grace and forgiveness keeps bitterness, revenge, and anger from destroying your marriage. It is not easy by any stretch of the imagination.

As we give to one another the acceptance and forgiveness that God has given to us, he brings that same redemption into our marriages. In bearing with one another and covering each other's sin with grace, God touches our lives together with healing.

Let's Talk About It

1. Why do you think spouses are often afraid to confess their sins or admit their faults?

2. What needs to happen in your marriage so that it's safe to be more open and forgiving? What is true in your marriage that has helped you become more transparent and forgiving?

3. How can your spouse pray for you now and in the coming week?

Prayer

Heavenly Father, thank you for your grace and forgiveness. Thank you for forgiving us when we don't deserve it. We pray that in our marriage we can forgive each other just as you forgive us. Help us to extend your grace to one another.

(Record any insights and decisions in the Journal section.)

● ● ●

Devotional Date #26

Those who refresh others will themselves be refreshed.

Proverbs 11:25

. . . .

Becoming a host in your marriage is challenging when there is deep hurt and resentment. If you go for long periods without attention, acceptance, affection, or admiration, you can easily become vulnerable to moodiness, retaliation, or rejection. It may not always be convenient or easy to reach out to your spouse.

The challenge is to show your love by serving, even when you do not feel like it. As you choose to love in this way, the feelings will come and your spouse is more likely to respond in the same manner.

I heard Dr. Gary Chapman, author of *The Five Love Languages*, tell about the way he learned to make the principle of servanthood practical in his marriage. As he struggled through a difficult time, he discovered that he lacked an attitude of servanthood. He made demands of his wife, expecting her to make him happy. His marriage changed when he asked his wife three questions:

- How can I help you?
- How can I make your life easier?
- How can I be a better husband to you?

Their marriage was transformed when he let her teach him how he could serve her. It did not happen overnight, because the pain had been there too long, but change did occur.

What will happen if your spouse is not actively serving in a host role in your marriage? Your first reaction may be to do the same thing. That will get his or her attention, you reason. There is no guarantee of that. Your second reaction may be to look outside your marriage.

While others can meet these needs, be careful of emotional attachments that may develop with someone of the opposite sex. Adulterous affairs do not always begin with a physical, sexual attraction. Instead, they begin when someone touches an emotional vacuum that is not filled in the marriage. Emotional affairs are very real and damaging to the covenant of marriage.

Instead of focusing on what you are missing, consider being proactive in loving your spouse. Take a step back for a moment and examine your marriage. Forget what you need or want, and focus on the expressed needs of your spouse. Make an honest assessment as to whether you are doing everything, within reason, to meet those needs. While you may be in need of emotional refreshing, consider this wise observation, "Those who refresh others will themselves be refreshed" (Proverbs 11:25). You must learn to surrender your doubts and insecurities, and take a big step outside of your comfort zone.

As you serve your spouse in a humble and gentle way, you will find refreshment in doing the right thing.

Let's Talk About It

1. Do you sometimes find it difficult to let your spouse serve you? Why? What could be done to help you grow in this area?

2. What do you think would be the greatest benefit for your marriage if you and your spouse became better servants of each other?

3. How can your spouse pray for you now and in the coming week?

Prayer

Heavenly Father, we pray that you would transform our hearts to be servant hearts, especially towards each other. Inspire us with creative ways to love, respect, honor, and cherish one another. May we experience a joy like never before.

(Record any insights and decisions in the Journal section.)

Devotional Date #27

However, each one of you must love his wife as he loves himself,
and the wife must respect her husband.

Ephesians 5:33

. . . .

L ove and respect in marriage is not an option for the Christian couple. It is a command of Scripture, without any exemption, as seen in the passage above. To honor and respect your spouse is not based on whether or not he or she has earned it. It is based on the fact that God considers your spouse worthy of Jesus' sacrificial death on the cross. Even when a spouse is not a Christian, he or she deserves respect and love because God values them.

Men report that they are motivated and encouraged in their marriages when they feel respected by their wives. When his wife does not respect him, a husband gradually becomes passive and less energized. With each passing day, he has less desire to actively engage his wife in the relationship. On the other hand, when he feels respected and trusted, he will do his best to fulfill his wife's needs. When he feels appreciated for his efforts, even when they fall short of her expectations, he will invest more of himself in their marriage.

Women report that in marriage they are motivated and encouraged when they feel cherished. When a woman does not feel cherished and honored by her husband, she is convinced he does not love her. There is a big hole in her heart. Dr. Emerson Eggerichs notes that a wife will spend her energy trying to change her husband by her loving criticism and complaints. When she feels loved and cherished by her husband, she is fulfilled and has more to give to their marriage.

The lack of respect and love in a marriage is evident in the following signs of a disappearing relationship:

- *Busyness* – This leads to neglect.

- *Avoidance* – You fail to confront the small relational snags until they have grown so large they are quenching your love and respect for each other.

- *Forgetfulness* – You disregard the small bonding behaviors that help your love grow and remain exciting.

- *Nit-picking* – You fail to overlook the unimportant flaws, unintentional slights, and minor blunders that occur in all friendships.

Does this list hit too close to home in your marriage? If so, the first step in cherishing and respecting your spouse is to reverse these damaging actions in your marriage. The next step is to boldly go where few are willing to go. Apologize to your spouse and ask for his or her forgiveness.

As you both take responsibility for how you treat each other, you will protect the love in your marriage.

Let's Talk About It

1. How has God spoken to your heart through this Devotional Date?

2. What does love look like to you? What does respect look like?

3. How can your spouse pray for you now and in the coming week?

Prayer

Heavenly Father, we pray that you would help us to love and respect at all times. May our speech be seasoned with it and may our actions reflect it, especially in those critical times when we may be at odds with each other.

(Record any insights and decisions in the Journal section.)

Devotional Date #28

How delightful is your love, my sister, my bride! How much more pleasing is your love than wine.

Song of Songs 4:10

. . . .

The *urge to merge* is from God, who intends it to be a fulfilling experience in marriage. In his infinite wisdom, God personally and lovingly created us male and female. He designed us so that we could enjoy within marriage the complete expression of the sexual dimension.

Great sex does not begin with soft lights, mood music, perfect bodies, and all the right moves. In a great marriage, sex begins with right thinking in your mind about marital intimacy.

How do you spell intimacy? Men tend to define it as some form of action, such as sexual intercourse, participating together in a recreational activity, and physically doing something for his wife. As one husband said to his wife, "What do you mean we need more intimacy? I just built you a gazebo!" That action increased the emotional bond he felt with his wife. He would not have done that for just any woman.

Women tend to view intimacy as the sharing of an emotional bond, warmth, closeness, and vulnerability. This is accomplished most often through meaningful heart-to-heart conversations. One wife complained about her husband when she said, "He tells me things that sound like a news report rather than loving thoughts." A man who is open about his own thoughts and feelings creates an emotional bond with his wife.

This difference between the sexes undeniably influences the physical expression of intimacy in marriage. David Olson, one of the authors of *Empowering Couples*, notes this distinction when he observes that feelings of emotional intimacy in the relationship usually precede sexual expression for women, whereas males often view sex as a way to increase intimacy. This variation on intimacy is responsible for more than a few marital skirmishes.

Rather than ignoring or fighting these differences, couples in great marriages are proactive in building an exclusive emotional and physical bond in their marriage. They realize that when you can relax and feel safe with each other, the stage is set for a more meaningful love life.

Furthermore, as a part of his good creation, God designed sexual pleasure for marriage. Proverbs instructs husbands to "rejoice in the wife of your youth...may her breasts satisfy you always, may you ever be captivated by her love" (Proverbs 5:18-19).

The marriage bed should be fun! Some people are so serious about *the objective*; they have lost the fun of the relationship. Grins, giggles, and laughter ought to be a part of your sexual intimacy.

Let's Talk About It

1. Has sex been more of a blessing or a burden in your marriage? Explain your answer.

2. What is one small thing you can do to improve your love life?

3. How can your spouse pray for you now and in the coming week?

Prayer

Heavenly Father, release us from the faulty ways we've viewed intimacy and sex in our marriage. Give us the courage to trust your plan for healthy sexuality in our marriage. Awaken our senses so that we can delight in each other's bodies as a means of glorifying you in our marriage.

(Record any insights and decisions in the Journal section.)

Devotional Date #29

The marriage bed must be a place of mutuality - the husband seeking to satisfy his wife, the wife seeking to satisfy her husband. Marriage is not a place to "stand up for your rights." Marriage is a decision to serve the other, whether in bed or out.

1 Corinthians 7:3-4 (THE MESSAGE)

. . . .

Have you approached sex in marriage as something you deserve and want? On the other hand, have you approached sex as a very wonderful way to please your spouse like no other person can?

The marriage bed is for the expression of unselfish affection. It's not all about you and your pleasure. Great sex in marriage happens when you focus on how to satisfy your spouse. This is the essence of what I call *The Principle of Satisfaction* based on the Bible passage above.

Marital intimacy is not just for your satisfaction. You are to discover what pleases your spouse and delight in fulfilling those desires. This means the marriage bed can still be exciting after many years of marriage because the husband and wife are still learning how to please one another.

The Old Testament also highlights *The Principle of Satisfaction* as seen in these verses:

- *Let him kiss me with the kisses of his mouth – for your love is more delightful than wine.* – Song of Songs 1:2

- *How delightful is your love, my sister, my bride! How much more pleasing is your love than wine.* – Song of Songs 4:10

The love mentioned in these verses refers to a married couple's physical intimacy – their caresses, embraces and consummation. These expressions of love were more delightful and more pleasing to them than any other experience in their lives. I was teaching on this topic in a marriage seminar and asked the couples to tell their spouses what they would substitute for wine in those passages. A husband later told me that his wife looked alluringly at him and whispered, "Chocolate." He was already thinking of some creative ways to make it more delightful for her.

We each are motivated differently when it comes to the marriage bed. Ladies, your husband is pleased when you are intentional about lovemaking and enjoy it yourself, when you express admiration of him as a husband and as a man, when you delight in his body, and when you create adventure and variety in lovemaking.

Men, your wife finds the marriage bed delightful when there is trust and emotional intimacy between the two of you, when there is respect and open communication, and when non-sexual affection is expressed both in and out of the marriage bed. You will spur her on with your generous love, acceptance, praise, and appreciation.

Let's Talk About It

1. How much do you think selfishness affects the average married couple regarding their sex life? In what ways can an attitude of servanthood transform a couple's love life?

2. What three things can your spouse do to encourage you as a lover?

3. How can your spouse pray for you now and in the coming week?

Prayer

Heavenly Father, we thank you for the holy desire you have given us for each other. Help us discover or rediscover what it is that satisfies each other in our love life. Set us free from selfishness. By your presence and power, keep our union pure and holy in every way.

(Record any insights and decisions in the Journal section.)

Devotional Date #30

The marriage bed must be a place of mutuality - the husband seeking to satisfy his wife, the wife seeking to satisfy her husband. Marriage is not a place to "stand up for your rights." Marriage is a decision to serve the other, whether in bed or out.

1 Corinthians 7:3-4 (THE MESSAGE)

. . . .

In a scene from an old Woody Allen movie (*Annie Hall*), a marriage counselor separately questions a husband and wife. The counselor asks the wife, "How often do you and your husband have sex?" She responds, "Almost always. Three times a week." The counselor then asks the husband, "How often do you and your wife have sex?" He responds, "Almost never. Three times a week."

Most spouses do not have the same need for physical affection and sexual intimacy. Typically, one desires to make love more frequently than the other one does. There is nothing wrong with that. Additionally, the man is not always the one who has the need for greater frequency. A young husband wrote, "Our sexual adjustment is very good, but my dear wife seems to have no idea that there are limits to a man's interest in sex. The few times I have tried to signal her to slow things down she seemed confused and hurt. Sex is great, but how do I introduce some moderation into the proceedings?" Many men reading this probably wonder why this guy is complaining.

Instead of fighting about frequency, you can practice *The Principle of Satisfaction* by honoring your spouse's desire for sexual intimacy. Your spouse will be happy. You will be happy. This is not a license to make unreasonable demands of each other. There will be times when sickness, fatigue, and the stresses of life will require a rain check.

Your level of satisfaction will also increase when you take the time to understand what affects your sexual relationship. Your spouse's lack of sexual desire may not have anything to do with you. As stated earlier, your natural desire for sexual union must get over some hurdles that keep you from the love life you both crave. Take time to communicate openly about what affects your love life. A complete medical checkup can be valuable. It will also be helpful for you to deal with emotional problems, past events and relationships, hurt feelings, bitterness, and poor self-image. Contact your pastor, a Christian counselor, or a mature couple to help you work through these matters.

Another positive thing you can do is to resolve major conflicts effectively, which will not give bitterness an opportunity to take root. Couples are often surprised how quickly their sex life deteriorates when love is lost in conflict and hatred. Your sexual intimacy can be a powerful reflection of how things are going in other areas of your relationship.

Let's Talk About It

1. In what ways has your past had a negative or positive impact on your marriage's sexuality?

2. What are the challenges to lovemaking in your marriage? What are some positive ways to overcome those challenges?

3. How can your spouse pray for you now and in the coming week?

Prayer

Heavenly Father, please help us to make our marriage a safe place where we can cultivate openness, honesty, and trust. By your power, heal any emotional wounds that may have a damaging effect on our love life. Help us to enjoy meaningful and intimate times with each other.

(Record any insights and decisions in the Journal section.)

Devotional Date #31

Your word is a lamp for my feet, a light on my path.

Psalms 119:105

. . . .

Weddings are filled with hopes, promises, celebrations, and dreams of living happily ever after. Those are good things. However, too many couples build their relationships on myths that they have either created in their own minds or read in some newsstand magazine article. Let's look at some of the more popular ones.

Myth #1: Happiness is the main purpose of marriage. If you think that God instituted marriage simply as a means of making you happy, then it's easy to walk away from a marriage that doesn't make you happy. God wants you and your spouse to work together to overcome whatever problems might be causing you to be unhappy with each other. No relationship is happy all the time. The supreme purpose of marriage is the blending of one man and one woman into an unbroken cord of unity and intimacy.

Myth #2: My commitment to Christ will guarantee that my marriage will work. Your commitment to Christ is a powerful tool for working through the challenges of life as a couple. Your marriage is stronger when you are both believers and rely upon the power of the Holy Spirit. However, God does not force people to respond to each other in a godly manner. Just because you are a Christian doesn't guarantee that your spouse will be one or act like one. It takes two people to make a marriage work.

Myth #3: If our relationship takes hard work, we must not be right for each other. Some people think that good relationships happen spontaneously. The truth is that anything that looks effortless generally takes a great deal of work. Watching two people ice skate at the Olympics may look effortless. However, what we see is the result of days, weeks, months, and years of practice that went into perfecting the routine. Old-fashioned hard work and perseverance are major components of a lasting marriage.

Myth #4: If my spouse and I do not always feel love for each other that means our relationship is in trouble. Love is more than a feeling. Feelings of romance come and go. The deeper aspects of true love transcend feelings and have more to do with commitment than emotion. The happiest couples are friends who share their lives in the daily habits of life. According to research by David Popenoe, happy couples define their marriage as a creation that has taken hard work and dedication. They have a long-lasting commitment to each other and the institution of marriage.

Let's Talk About It

1. How have marriage myths (these or others) influenced your expectations in marriage?

2. How can your spouse pray for you now and in the coming week?

Prayer

Father, guide us into all truth. Teach us to obey your Word and build our marriage on your truth, not on myths that deceive. Help us to stand perfect and complete in your truth, knowing who we are in Christ and submitting daily to your design for marriage.

(Record any insights and decisions in the Journal section.)

Devotional Date #32

Above all, love each other deeply, because love covers over a multitude of sins...Humble yourselves, therefore, under God's mighty hand, that he may lift you up in due time. Cast all your anxiety on him because he cares for you.

1 Peter 4:8; 5:6-7

. . . .

Many, if not all, married couples have had their friendship stretched. You do not have to be married long before stormy weather attempts to capsize your marriage boat.

A man had just bought a boat and kept it in a harbor on the coast of Florida. A hurricane was brewing and was about to hit land. He did not know what to do. He had made a sizable investment in this boat and he did not want to lose it. A friend, who had experience with boats and hurricanes, gave him this advice, "Don't attempt to tie the boat to the dock or anything on land. It will be torn to pieces. Your only hope is to anchor deep. Take four anchors and drop them deep. The boat will be able to ride out the storm."

I believe there at least four anchors that can keep your marriage from being torn apart in stormy weather.

Anchor #1: Trust God – To keep your marriage from crashing on the rocks, daily submit to God's guidance for your lives and marriage. Trust that God knows what is best for you. The indispensable basis for an enduring, unwavering, and joyful commitment to building a great marriage in stormy weather is an implicit faith in God's goodness. I stake my life on the certain truth that God would never ask us, his children, to go through anything that does not have our well-being in view.

Anchor #2: Love Each Other Deeply – In stormy weather, give top priority to maintaining a loving relationship with each other. Turn toward each other to provide a shelter in the storm. Make your relationship with your spouse a priority during times of strain and struggle. Keep doing the things that express love and friendship – fun dates, casual walks, and meaningful conversations.

Anchor #3: Let God Shape You – God uses stormy weather to shape and mold us into the image of Jesus Christ. If we refuse to change how we think and relate to one another, the anchor line will snap and our marriage boat will begin to flounder.

Anchor #4: Persevere in Faithfulness – In your marriage vows, you promised to remain faithful regardless of all the changes and adversities, regardless of good times, bad times, wealth or poverty. You promised to persevere with each other through the changing seasons of life.

To keep your marriage from crashing on the rocks, be prepared to anchor deep with these four anchors.

Let's Talk About It

1. How have difficulties in your life served as an instrument of growth for you individually and as a couple?

2. Are you facing stormy weather now? Which anchor(s) do you need to focus on?

3. How can your spouse pray for you now and in the coming week?

Prayer

Father, we pray for the strength to endure the more difficult seasons of our life together; strength to endure the days that bring us down emotionally and physically. Please guide us in how to comfort and love each other, especially when hard times hit. May your joy carry us through the stormy weather.

(Record any insights and decisions in the Journal section.)

Devotional Date #33

His mouth is altogether sweet; he is lovely in every way. Such, O women of Jerusalem, is my lover, my friend.

Song of Songs 5:16

. . . .

Through the years of our marriage, we developed a friendship of mutual affection, rapport, and solidarity. It did not automatically appear when we said our vows and exchanged rings. Our friendship grew and matured as we practiced these six habits.

Friends stay in touch with each other. Friendship implies a relationship in which all parties involved make consistent efforts to maintain. To neglect these efforts is to risk allowing the relationship to wither and possibly disappear entirely. We verbally communicate with each other in a way that says, "I am interested in you as a person."

Friends share themselves and their experiences. Without this level of sharing, you may have an acquaintance, but you do not have a friend. Sharing thoughts, feelings, and experiences creates an openness that deepens the bond. Spouses who have grown apart share only negative emotions. Their cynical or critical thoughts focus only on problems and frustrations.

Friends are supportive during troubled times. Friends must always be there for one another, not only during the good times, but also during times of emotional turmoil or personal crisis. To have such a friend in times of need is a wonderful source of strength. What helps me get through my troubled times is when Cindy gives me a hug and tells me she is confident that we will get through this.

Friends consistently affirm one another. Good friends communicate a very simple message: "I like you, and being with you makes me feel good." Friends communicate regularly in small acts of kindness and loving words. On one of our wedding anniversaries, Cindy gave me a card with the following statement: "It's one thing to be in love. It's another to be good friends. And it's a wonderful thing to be madly in love with my best friend!" That's affirming!

Deep trust always exists between friends. As friendship deepens, a corresponding openness about experiences and feelings develops. To deepen our trust we will not use a personal sensitivity to hurt each other when we are angry. We do not gossip about each other because it is a betrayal of marital trust.

Friends let go and have fun together. Friends enjoy good times together knowing that they will be there for one another when tough times come. As married life becomes busier, humor often fades, and no time remains for fun. Stressed and tired, couples feel overwhelmed with responsibilities. Fun is a powerful tool in relieving stress.

A special friendship is vital to a great marriage. Why just be married when you can be married to your best friend?

Let's Talk About It

1. What does friendship mean to you? How does that compare to the habits listed above?

2. What can you do to deepen the friendship in your marriage?

3. How can your spouse pray for you now and in the coming week?

Prayer

Father, we thank you for bringing us together. We pray that you would intensify the bonds of friendship in our marriage. May your creativity stimulate us to love each other like never before.

(Record any insights and decisions in the Journal section.)

Devotional Date #34

"Haven't you read the Scriptures?" Jesus replied. "They record that from the beginning 'God made them male and female.' And he said, 'This explains why a man leaves his father and mother and is joined to his wife, and the two are united into one.' Since they are no longer two but one, let no one split apart what God has joined together."

Matthew 19:4-6 (NLT)

. . . .

It seems that the primary goal in relationships today is personal gratification. What's in it for me? Will all of my needs be met? If the relationship no longer meets their personal needs, they move on to one that will.

Is this the purpose of marriage? From a biblical standpoint, marriage cannot be reduced to a mere sharing of the same bed or the same house. Two people can live in the same rooms, use the same bathroom, have sexual intercourse, and still come short of the purpose for which God established marriage. The purpose of marriage revolves around four goals.

To mirror God's image. (Genesis 1:26-27) In many ways, marriage mirrors the relationship between the Father, Son, and Holy Spirit. Relationship is at the very core of the nature of the Trinity. Each member of the Trinity complements one another perfectly, and as the Godhead are "one." Yet, each plays a unique role in the Divine plan of the universe. In marriage, each spouse plays a unique role in God's plan for the family, yet they are to be "one flesh." A couple's oneness reflects the character and unity of God.

To complement and complete one another. (Genesis 2:18) Although it has been fashionable at times to think that there are no real differences between men and women, volumes of research and common sense prove otherwise. We are equal in worth, but different in design. In the union of a man and a woman, we complement and complete each other as God designed – physically, psychologically, emotionally and spiritually.

To serve one another as an illustration of the relationship between Christ and the church. (Ephesians 5:25-33) Marriage is a laboratory for developing God's love in you. He will use your spouse to build his values, attitudes, morals, and character within you. Once you understand this, a lot of what happens within your marriage will begin to make more sense. You might be asking, "Why is this happening to me?" The answer is – to make you more like Jesus!

To multiply a godly legacy. (Genesis 1:28a) Marriage provides a healthy and safe context for having and rearing children. God created family in such a way that it is the primary learning environment for children. By watching Mom and Dad, they learn to love others and to appreciate their spiritual, emotional and sexual identity.

God's plan for you and your spouse—for your marriage—is wider and deeper than anything in your wildest, craziest dreams.

Let's Talk About It

1. How do these goals reflect your purpose for marriage?

2. How can you more intentionally achieve God's purpose for marriage?

3. How can your spouse pray for you now and in the coming week?

Prayer

Father, we thank you for the blessings you are pouring out on our marriage. May our union reflect your purpose for marriage as we relate to one another in ways that honor you. Help us to align our hearts and goals with your purposes.

(Record any insights and decisions in the Journal section.)

Devotional Date #35

So in everything, do to others what you would have them do to you,
for this sums up the Law and the Prophets. (Jesus)

Matthew 7:12

. . . .

Have you ever wondered what it's like to be your spouse? What it's like to wear a coat and tie every day even in the heat of July? Or to wear a skirt in the frigid winds of February? Or to relocate for your partner's career and feel like your identity got lost in the move? How about what it's like to spend hours to plan, shop for, and prepare a meal that will be eaten in less than 15 minutes? Or to spend all afternoon working on the car and then be accused of doing nothing around the house? Or perhaps you wonder what it's like to come home from a stressful day at work to meet a spouse who is equally stressed?

Imagining what it's like to walk in your spouse's shoes is a valuable tool for building a great marriage. It's called *empathy*, which is the ability to accurately see the world through your spouse's eyes.

The effect of mutual empathy in marriage is staggering. Research has shown that 90 percent of our misunderstandings would be resolved if we did nothing more than see that issue from our partner's perspective.

Take a moment to immerse yourself in your spouse's world. Do your best to imagine what it would be like to be living in his or her skin. Next, consider a typical day and ask yourself questions like these: What would you worry about? What would be your likely stress points? What would bring you the greatest joy or satisfaction? Would you have different financial responsibilities or pressures? Would you feel more or less self-assured? How would you feel about your spouse (that would be you!)? What would you want most from your spouse?

Jesus recognized the extreme value of empathy: "Do for others what you would like them to do for you. This is a summary of all that is taught in the law and the prophets" (Matthew 7:12, NLT). What a great maxim for marriage!

Empathy begins with an awareness of another person's feelings. It would be easier to be aware of other people's emotions if they would simply tell us how they felt. However, since most people do not, we must ask questions, reading between the lines, guessing, and trying to interpret non-verbal cues. Emotionally expressive people are easiest to read because their eyes and faces are constantly letting us know how they are feeling.

Once we have figured out how another person feels, we show empathy by acknowledging the emotion. We can also show empathy through a simple sign of affection such as hug or a tender touch. Though empathy often refers to sensing someone else's painful feelings, it can also apply to someone's positive feelings of success, accomplishment, pride, and achievement. In this case, a "high five" would also be a sign of empathy.

Let's Talk About It

1. In what areas do you struggle to empathize with your spouse? What would help you to better relate to your spouse's life circumstances?

2. How can your spouse pray for you now and in the coming week?

Prayer

Lord, we ask that the love you have implanted in our hearts will always inspire us to be kind in our words, considerate of feelings, and concerned for each other's needs and wishes. Help us to be understanding and forgiving.

(Record any insights and decisions in the Journal section.)

Devotional Date #36

My dear brothers and sisters, be quick to listen, slow to speak, and slow to get angry. Human anger does not produce the righteousness God desires.

James 1:19-20 (NLT)

. . . .

Anger is not all together a bad emotion. What you do with your anger determines whether it becomes a problem. Like the warning lights that go off on your car dashboard, anger is telling you there is a problem that needs your attention. However, if you ignore the warning too long, your problem can quickly become a disaster.

As an emotion, anger can range from intense rage to minor irritation. The easiest way to know if you are angry is to take notice of your body. If your heart rate increases, blood starts pumping, and your breathing is exaggerated, you are angry. An impulse to retaliate usually accompanies anger. The retaliation side of anger creates the disconnection in your marriage.

Anger is most often a response to one of the following: a hurt from the past; frustration in the present moment; and fear or anxiety about the future. Each of these creates some kind of pain for us and our self-protective instinct is to put up a "deflector shield" resulting in anger.

Anger is not a primary emotion. It is a secondary emotion. There is always something underneath the anger. When you have feelings of anger, you would do well to ask yourself the question, "What am I hurt about, frustrated about, or afraid of?" Then address that issue.

I learned from Gary Smalley that the external problem is rarely the problem. If you are feeling angry, then you can count on the fact that one of your hot buttons is being pushed. The more you understand why you are angry, the more you can control how you react after becoming angry.

Whether your anger is legitimate or distorted, do not condemn yourself for experiencing the anger. Anger itself is not sinful. How you act on your anger could be sinful. (Ephesians 4: 26-27) Do not give others the power to control your feelings. Take control of your thoughts, feelings, and actions. You can choose to be angry or you can choose another reaction or emotion.

You are responsible for how you react when someone pushes your buttons. Blaming your spouse or others is one of the largest factors in causing imbalance in your relationships and keeping the anger going. By taking responsibility, you take back control and you are able to let go of all kinds of resentments. Resentment inevitably affects our well-being and always bounces back on us.

Remember that anger is a secondary emotion. If you try to deal just with the anger, you are dealing with symptoms, not the root of the behavior. Look for the primary cause or focus of your anger.

Let's Talk About It

1. What are the major causes (hot buttons) of your anger?

2. The next time a potential angry explosion is about to erupt in your marriage, what are you going to do about it?

3. How can your spouse pray for you now and in the coming week?

Prayer

Lord, we ask you to help us to manage anger so it doesn't destroy our marriage. Help us to refrain from using anger as a weapon to hurt each other. May our hearts be so filled with your love and peace that there is no room for anger.

(Record any insights and decisions in the Journal section.)

• • •

Devotional Date #37

Yet I hold this against you: You have forsaken the love you had at first. Consider how far you have fallen! Repent and do the things you did at first.

Revelation 2:4-5

. . . .

How do you redevelop dedication and enthusiasm for a marriage whose light has dimmed? First, you need to believe that it can be done, especially with the Lord's help. I cannot predict the future of your relationship, but most couples are able to repair and strengthen a lifeless and frustrating marriage.

Second, you must be willing to work at it. It will take an unrelenting effort to restore the feelings of dedication and enthusiasm. Most likely, you will have to work against your present feelings and some negative tendencies that now exist in the relationship.

If you are willing to work at it, then the next thing to do is follow a strategy Jesus gave to the church at Ephesus in the Book of Revelation. (See Revelation 2:1-7). He says *remember, repent,* and *repeat* the things you did at first. How would this strategy look when applied to restoring the passion and dedication in a marriage?

Remember what you used to have together. Spend some time reminiscing about the good old days. What were things like when you first met? What attracted you to each other? What did you do on your first date? What kinds of things did you do for fun? Do you still do any of these things? Although it can make you feel sad, most couples find this kind of reminiscing enjoyable and enlightening. It can be fun to remember the good old days. Beware of the tendency to rewrite history. Some people view past experiences in a negative light, even though they were actually positive at the time. You can recapture some of the good feelings that once characterized your relationship. In some ways, this step is an attempt to regain an appetite or desire for the relationship again.

Repent and decide to turn things around. This is fundamentally a decision of your will to change your mind and your direction. Most people have enough control over their own lives to make a decision and stick with it when they want something badly enough. Repentance brings the Lord into the equation as you ask Him for help in turning things around.

Repeat the things you did at first. The point is simple but the impact can be profound. Early in a relationship, couples talk more as friends and do more fun things together. They are more forgiving and more likely to look for the good and not the bad in the other. They also do a better job of controlling conflict. The things you do to renew and restore life and energy in your marriage are the same things that couples do to prevent marital distress in the first place. What you must supply, with the Lord's help, is the willingness to act.

Let's Talk About It

1. Are there signs of losing your enthusiasm for your relationship? Identify them.

2. What are you going to do to renew you dedication and enthusiasm for your marriage?

3. How can your spouse pray for you now and in the coming week?

Prayer

Lord, may your Holy Spirit transform us and teach us to care for one another in humility and gentleness. Inspire our intimacy, drawing us close, and fill our marriage with a renewed dedication and energy to have the marriage of our dreams.

(Record any insights and decisions in the Journal section.)

Devotional Date #38

Fix your thoughts on what is true and honorable and right. Think about things that are pure and lovely and admirable. Think about things that are excellent and worthy of praise.

Philippians 4:8 (NLT)

. . . .

You cannot always change your environment, but you can change your attitude. The day after a heavy rain, you can look down and see puddles and mud, or look up and see a beautiful sky. It's a change of perspective.

A key element to a healthy, strong marriage is the attitude you both have about your marriage. The attitude that you and your spouse choose to have, on a daily basis, will greatly influence the life you enjoy together. Negative attitudes can create a tremendous weight on your marriage, while a consistently positive attitude can help uplift your marriage – putting everything in its real perspective.

Your attitude – how you think about your spouse and what you think about your spouse – is powerful because it determines your feelings and actions. It's easy to be negative in marriage, which makes it even more necessary that you focus on your spouse's good qualities and express thanks with positive words.

If you are expecting and anticipating that your spouse is going to be complaining, that is what you are going to hear. Since you are expecting it, it will be what stands out most when your spouse speaks to you. If you expect your spouse to be dissatisfied with you, then you are going to prepare an appropriate (or inappropriate) response in advance, even when that might not have been your intention.

When you think negative thoughts or expect negative responses, you develop a negative attitude. Attitude is what you get after you develop a style of thinking (positive or negative) and then practice it so well that it seems like you don't even have to think it out before you respond. Having an attitude is like pre-thinking your next response.

A positive attitude requires a clear action plan that addresses your thoughts and words. Here are three affirmations that you can use to build a better attitude about your marriage:

1. I will not be a complainer!

2. I will speak to myself with encouraging words! I will speak aloud things that God says are true, regardless of how I feel.

3. Every time I think of my spouse, I will pray, "Lord, thank you for giving my husband/wife as your awesome gift. Help me to see the great value of your gift to me!"

Let's Talk About It

1. What do you think about this statement? – "You cannot always change your environment, but you can change your attitude."

2. How has your attitude about yourself and/or your spouse played either a positive or a negative role in your marriage?

3. How can your spouse pray for you now and in the coming week?

Prayer

Lord, please help us to control our attitudes and to respond to each other with love and kindness. Transform our minds to be aware of what triggers these attitudes and how to stop them. May our attitudes reflect your character always.

(Record any insights and decisions in the Journal section.)

Devotional Date #39

But those who marry will face many troubles in this life.

1 Corinthians 7:28

. . . .

How do you react to stress in your marriage? Some people take everything in stride. Their naturally laid-back attitude shines through even in stressful situations. Another deadline? Bring it on. The dishwasher is leaking? No problem. It will be a simple repair. Others get anxious at the first sign of a stressful situation. Running late for a meeting? Time to panic! Stuck in a traffic jam? Let the cursing begin!

Using healthy coping mechanisms can help couples respond to stress in healthier ways. What can you and your spouse do if you react to stress in negative ways?

Get your emotions out in a positive way. Bottling up emotions can have a huge impact on marriages. You might think that avoiding conflict is less stressful, but it usually causes both of you to store up tension. As tension grows, so does resentment, resulting in an even bigger argument. It is better to discuss things that make you unhappy in a respectful and calm way before letting them blow up.

Approach challenges with open communication. If there are issues that are troubling you, set aside a time to talk with each other in a relaxed setting. Be willing to share each other's concerns, fears and hopes without criticizing or judging. Talk about how you can work together to improve the situation. In order for a couple to work as a team, you need to know what your spouse is really thinking about the issue. Problems escalate when you stop talking with each other.

You don't always have to be right. Your spouse's opinion will be different from yours. No surprise there! Do not expect him or her to see things in the same light as you all the time. Learn to compromise and realize that there is not always a wrong or a right in a given situation. Both of you can have equally valid points of view.

Pray together. Bring to God in prayer the things that cause you stress. Ask him to help you discern what to do to ease the stress in your lives and to help you stay committed to your marriage.

Show your affection. Make it a point to tell each other "I love you," and say it often. Do not assume your spouse knows your feelings at the moment. It's during the tough times that your partner needs the reassurance of your love even more.

Plan for couple time. Carve out time in your schedule, several times a week, to be alone with your mate and get away from whatever is causing you stress. Take a walk together. Go out to dinner. Have a picnic at the park. Get up a half hour earlier so that you and your spouse can have a quiet breakfast in bed before you leave for work. Share a pot of tea after the kids are in bed. If you cannot fit couple time into your busy schedule, you need to reprioritize your time commitments so that you can.

Let's Talk About It

1. How do you typically respond to stress?

2. Which suggestions above will help you minimize stress in your marriage?

3. How can your spouse pray for you now and in the coming week?

Prayer

Lord, protect, preserve, and sustain our marriage in the stress-filled times of our lives. Do not allow difficulties or the enemy to separate what you have joined together.

(Record any insights and decisions in the Journal section.)

Devotional Date #40

I know your deeds, that you are neither cold nor hot...you are lukewarm.

Revelation 3:15-16

. . . .

A cold marriage has no romance. Dating is nonexistent. The wife prefers hanging out with her friends and the husband dreads going home. Either spouse may spend more time at work than at home because work is more fulfilling. More often than not, if you have an unresolved conflict, one of you opts to sleep in another room. Finally, your conflicts may linger for weeks or even months. It is at this stage that one or both of you may start thinking about divorce. You argue daily and remain together because of the children, your finances (you may not be able to survive on your own), or you are afraid of what your family and friends will think if you tell them you are filing for divorce.

Somewhere between hot and cold is the lukewarm marriage. It's not bad, but it's not great either. Some describe it as comfortable. It becomes more like having a roommate or a business partner who lives in the house. There is very little passion, if any. The excitement is gone. It is no longer satisfying and fun.

Sometimes people settle for a mediocre marriage. They think it is good enough and that everyone else they know is "in the same boat." They resign themselves to a life of feeling bored with their partner. They may say things such as, "At least she's a good mother" or "He's a hard worker and doesn't get drunk." However, the passion and fire are gone.

What is wrong with having a "good enough" marriage? The reason is that these marriages are just one or two steps away from disaster at all times. A weak marriage is far more susceptible to affairs and divorce due to neglect.

To keep love alive and strong in your marriage, give top priority to maintaining a loving relationship with your spouse. Elements of a *hot* marriage would be things like weekly dates for fun, special romantic nights at home, leisurely walks in the park, relaxing chats about nonsense, and settling disagreements immediately. The bottom line is that you just enjoy being in your spouse's company.

Let's Talk About It

1. How would you describe your marriage: Hot? Cold? Lukewarm?

2. Is anything getting in the way of your marriage? If so, what is it and what can you do about it?

3. How can your spouse pray for you now and in the coming week?

Prayer

Heavenly Father, keep our hearts pure and our minds engaged so that we might find great delight and joy in each other. Create within us a hunger for each other and a desire to have the best marriage possible. May we find pleasure in each other and do all we can with your help to keep our marriage alive.

(Record any insights and decisions in the Journal section.)

Devotional Date #41

Don't push your way to the front; don't sweet-talk your way to the top. Put yourself aside, and help others get ahead. Don't be obsessed with getting your own advantage. Forget yourselves long enough to lend a helping hand.

Philippians 2:3-4 (THE MESSAGE)

. . . .

The eighteenth-century French philosopher, Joseph Joubert, said, "The aim of an argument or discussion should not be victory, but progress." When one spouse in a marriage loses, both spouses lose. The marriage suffers. A *No-Losers Policy* helps you work toward mutual understanding and a win-win solution.

In great marriages, couples recognize the enormous value of teamwork. Each spouse is committed to working on cooperative strategies. A marriage dies when selfishness replaces teamwork as the motivation for resolving disagreements. The setting aside of your own agenda, for the benefit of your spouse, is required at significant moments in marriage, as noted in the Bible passage above.

Hard pushing competitiveness may help you become the sales person of the month, land that new job, or win a sports contest. It will not help you build a great marriage. Power struggles in marriage are destructive. Why? In every power struggle, people become adversaries, trying to crush their opponent. You view your spouse as the enemy who must be defeated at all costs.

Your spouse is not your enemy! Zig Ziglar, a popular motivational speaker, once remarked, "Many marriages would be better if the husband and wife clearly understood that they are on the same side." God's plan for a great marriage is for husbands and wives to be a team, united in accomplishing his purposes in marriage. Jesus emphasized this marital unity in one of his conversations with the Pharisees:

Haven't you read…that at the beginning the Creator "made them male and female," and said, "For this reason a man will leave his father and mother and be united to his wife, and the two will become one flesh"? So they are no longer two, but one. Therefore what God has joined together, let man not separate. – Matthew 19:4-6

Dr. Howard Hendricks, a noted author and speaker, said that one of the things he learned from working with the Dallas Cowboys football players was the importance of the team. "When you are on a team," he said, "you play off the strengths of your teammates. You don't tackle the guys who wear the same color uniforms."

Having to win every argument will wear you down physically, emotionally, and spiritually. It will also destroy your marriage. There is a better way. Approach your disagreements with a desire to protect what is great about your marriage from whatever problem you are facing at the time.

Let's Talk About It

1. What do you like about a *No Losers Policy* in marriage?

2. What might be some challenges to maintaining such a policy in a marriage relationship?

3. How can your spouse pray for you now and in the coming week?

Prayer

Heavenly Father, teach us how to address things that hinder our relationship, that keep it from being all that you want it to be. Help us work through our differences with kindness and gentleness.

(Record any insights and decisions in the Journal section.)

Devotional Date #42

Dear friends, since God so loved us, we also ought to love one another. We love because he first loved us.

1 John 4:11, 19

. . . .

Love is greatly tested in our marriages. Those whom we love may choose to do things that hurt us greatly. Earl Palmer wrote, "We must love the real people in the real places where we live."

Marital love is not just for those who are pleasant to us or who are nice and easy-going. We are not to love because people are lovable or because they fit our mold of righteousness. The command is to love a person who is like us – with faults, imperfections, and hang-ups. You do not have to agree with them or condone their lifestyles, but you do have to love them.

This kind of love – love for imperfect people – is from God. God is this kind of love. God is love. Wherever the life of God is found, that love is found. If that love is not found, the life of God is not found in us.

What is your response to the stubbornness and rudeness of other people? Your spouse, for example. Does it make your blood boil? Does your temper explode with rants and ravings? What was God's response to our stubbornness and rebellion, to our imperfect hearts? Take a moment to read 1 John 4:9-11 in your Bible.

God showed his unconditional love through Jesus and the cross. His love resulted in Jesus breaking the shackles of fear, hate, and evil. He showed this love for us so that our quarreling and abuse would be replaced by patience, acceptance, and the power to remain calm in the midst of our flawed relationships.

If you have experienced the overwhelming cleansing of God's love for you, despite all of your flaws, you not only can love imperfect people, but you will want to love them. We can love imperfect people when we have within us the life of God through Jesus Christ.

God is the God of imperfect people – people who make mistakes, people whose lives are not perfect, people who have messed up, and people who stumble in many ways. When you let Jesus into your life, when you live like Jesus, the Holy Spirit enables you to love like Jesus. Where his life is, his love will be, because love always follows the life of God.

As long as we are nice to those who are nice to us, no one has any idea that God is around. However, when we return good for evil, when we are patient, tender, thoughtful, and considerate when others are stubborn, obstinate, and selfish, then people get the sense that God is somewhere close by. God's life in us becomes visible to them.

God's love reaches its ultimate completeness and perfection in us when it becomes visible in how we relate to our spouse who stumbles, like us, in many ways.

Let's Talk About It

1. What are two or three examples of how love has been tested in your relationship?

2. How have you seen God's love in your marriage?

3. How can your spouse pray for you now and in the coming week?

Prayer

Heavenly Father, your Word tells us that there is no fear in love. Perfect love drives out fear, because fear has to do with punishment. The one who fears is not made perfect in love. Create in us a heart filled with your love. As you have loved us, may we love others who stumble in many ways.

(Record any insights and decisions in the Journal section.)

Devotional Date #43

After I looked things over, I stood up and said to the nobles, the officials and the rest of the people, "Don't be afraid of them. Remember the Lord, who is great and awesome, and fight for your families, your sons and your daughters, your wives and your homes."

Nehemiah 4:14

. . . .

We all can reach a point where we may be ready to throw in the towel and give up. Tired, frustrated, and exhausted, we feel like there is no use in continuing to try. We cannot see any light at the end of the tunnel and wonder if we should just quit the fight. Have you been there before? Are you there today?

In today's Bible reading, we find Nehemiah's God-inspired response to a stressed-out group of people. They are fatigued, facing financial challenges, and surrounded by an enemy determined to undermine all they were doing. I strongly believe his challenge is relevant for our marriages and families.

First, he rebukes their fears. Fear is an emotion we all know and it influences many of our actions throughout life. When we are afraid, we lie, hide, run or stop and do not take action. Fear immobilizes. It puts us out of action. What usually happens is that fear puts images of failure in our minds. It paralyzes us and prevents us from fighting back. Nehemiah's rebuke calls the people back to a sense of what is true.

He then redirects their focus. Nehemiah does not speak to the impossibility of the task. He does not give credit to the power of their foes. Instead, he calls for a refocus. Remember God's love. Remember God's power. He is an awesome God, who is completely good, reliable and faithful. Typically, when we feel discouraged, we have our eyes on the problem and not the Lord. We need to remember our source for living in times of discouragement. God is the one who gives us the victory.

Finally, he renews their purpose. We can easily lose sight of our purpose in building our marriage and family relationships. Nehemiah knew that the battle was personal. The motivation was in the heart. "Fight for your brothers, yours sons and your daughters, your wives and your homes." How can you fight for your marriage? Be intentional and purposeful about what you want your marriage/family to be and where it is going. Maintain a watchful eye on what can weaken your relationships. Protect your home, your heart, your marriage, and your children from the corruption of this ungodly world.

Take a good look at your marriage. Is everything going well? Decide today to fight for your marriage and family. Do not give in to discouragement. Stand strong and fight for what matters!

Let's Talk About It

1. What can you and your spouse do to keep a watchful eye on threats to your marriage?

2. Does your marriage need refocusing? Explain.

3. How can your spouse pray for you now and in the coming week?

Prayer

Heavenly Father, our hope and strength are from you alone. You alone are our rock and our salvation. You are our fortress. We will not be shaken. Thank you for being our refuge and allowing us to pour out our hearts to you.

(Record any insights and decisions in the Journal section.)

Devotional Date # 44

A new command I give you: Love one another. As I have loved you, so you must love one another. By this everyone will know that you are my disciples, if you love one another.

John 13:34-35

. . . .

Arnie was nine or ten years old at the time I saw his story on television. He left home because his father laughed at him, beat him, and said that he talked funny. It was true. His mouth hung crooked on one side and he could not form his words well. He stumbled and slurred his speech regularly. He left home and lived in an alley in a large box, with his best friend, a cat named Thomas.

Arnie shoplifted some cat food for Thomas and some candles for himself. It was Arnie's birthday and he wanted to celebrate it with his best friend. He opened the cat food tin, placed the candles on top, and lit all of them. He closed his eyes and before he blew them out, he made a wish: "I wish that somebody would love me."

On the surface, your marriage may be running smoothly with little or no difficulty; however, something is missing if it is not fueled and nurtured by love. Jesus clearly teaches that love is a distinguishing feature of any relationship where he is present and his words are obeyed. What does that "love" look like in a healthy marriage relationship? There are at least three ways you can show love in your marriage.

The way in which you listen to each other. Refusing to listen becomes an obstacle to healthy relationships. Any problem, big or small, often begins with bad communication. Someone is not listening. Do you listen to what your spouse is saying, and what they are not saying? This is how we discover the true feelings. Refusing to listen reveals a lack of interest and genuine love.

The way in which you speak to each other. Oscar Wilde said that ultimately the bond of all companionship, whether in marriage or in friendship, is conversation. Is your conversation peppered with words of affirmation and encouragement? Are you honest and thoughtful in the way you speak to each other?

The way in which you involve yourselves in each other's lives. Marital researcher Frank Pittman said, "Marriage, like a submarine, is only safe if you get all the way inside." Loving each other means full involvement in life together. Make time to dream and plan together. Develop the habit of dating each other. Take regular getaways without the children. Give each other the freedom to grow and change. Continue to read, attend seminars, and educate yourselves about how to be better spouses and lovers. Make time for intimacy with your spouse.

An enduring and persevering love values the marriage relationship above selfish interests. How does your marriage measure up?

Let's Talk About It

1. On a scale of 1 to 10, with "1" being poor and "10" being terrific, how would you rate each of the three measurements of love in your marriage?

2. How can you increase each score by one or two points in the next week?

3. How can your spouse pray for you now and in the coming week?

Prayer

Heavenly Father, you are the essence of love. We know what love is because of your love for us. Help us to display a more genuine love for each other as we listen, speak, and live life together.

(Record any insights and decisions in the Journal section.)

Devotional Date #45

Make the most of every opportunity for doing good in these evil days.

Ephesians 5:16 (NLT)

. . . .

O ur first trip to Washington, D.C. was a logistical challenge for me. Not leaving anything to chance, I decided to scout out where I would be parking the car the next day. No problem. Easy!

After breakfast, we moved out into the rush-hour traffic, assured that my prearranged plans were flawless. Nearing the destination, I merged into the turning lane only to discover that someone had placed brightly colored wooden barriers in my path. "Where did those things come from? They weren't there last night!" The next thing I knew, the Lincoln Memorial, which had only been an intriguing structure in photographs, was looming before me. I was now driving into what the travel book described as hostile territory for first-time visitors.

Barriers have a way of popping up unexpectedly in many areas of our journey through life. Marriage is no exception. In our pursuit of the intimate marriage – a relationship where there is a sense of being unconditionally accepted, valued, and understood – barriers spring up to hinder our quest.

One such barrier is busyness. The demanding pressures and responsibilities of life can easily drive us into what Howard Hendricks called marriage morbidity – living together without closeness. As we scurry about to accomplish the mundane, we take each other for granted. A marriage falters if the only time the couple sees each other is when they are exhausted.

To remove this barrier, you must first evaluate your priorities in life. What is important to you? How do the choices you make reflect your priorities?

One husband discovered there was not enough time for his career, his marriage, his children, and personal leisure time. The result was that certain activities (such as golf, which takes hours away from home) were impossible at that time in his life. He decided to spend his personal time at home where he could be close to his wife and family.

Planning time together is critical to developing an intimate relationship. A couple in one of our marriage seminars said they mark out time for each other on their calendars. You can do this on a weekly or monthly basis. Another couple reserves the same day each week for their special time together. Some couples wash dishes together as they share their thoughts and life events. Others rise early in the morning to spend private moments together.

What can you do this week to moderate the busyness of your life? The intimacy of your marriage may be sidetracked if you do not make some changes.

Let's Talk About It

1. What are three major barriers to spending time together?

2. What can you do this week to moderate the busyness of your life?

3. How can your spouse pray for you now and in the coming week?

Prayer

Heavenly Father, we thank you for our marriage and for your presence in it. It is so easy to be sidetracked in the rush of our days and miss the very special opportunities to connect with you and with each other. Give us wisdom to know when we need to pull back from the busyness of life to keep our marriage strong.

(Record any insights and decisions in the Journal section.)

Devotional Date #46

Again, you have heard that it was said to the people long ago, "Do not break your oath, but fulfill to the Lord the vows you have made."

Matthew 5:33

. . . .

Many of us believe that love is the glue that holds a marriage together. It is certainly a major component. However, I think there is something else that contributes to a lasting bond – your promises to each other.

When performing a marriage ceremony, I ask the bride and groom if they promise to *love, comfort, honor and keep each other, in sickness and in health; and, forsaking all others, keep only unto him/her, so long as you both shall live.* I always get a resounding, "I do!"

The promises you made to each other – your vows – form a firm foundation upon which to build your marriage. As you go through the various seasons of your marriage, the significance of these promises becomes extraordinarily apparent. Let's examine briefly the promises to love, comfort, honor, and keep each other.

Love each other. The love promised better be a sacrificial love that knows how to put the needs of your spouse above your own. It is a love of action, not merely emotion, exercised as a choice of your will. We do not do what we do because we feel the way we feel. We feel the way we feel because we do what we do. When you promised to love your spouse, you offered a unique love to your partner, intended only for the two of you to share.

Comfort each other. This is a promise to care about your spouse in a gentle, supportive way. A million things can make life just a little bit harder. When this happens, you have to be there to comfort and encourage each other. It can be a listening ear or an embrace that says it all. It could be a word that communicates we will get through this. There are times when your spouse needs comfort and you do not feel like giving it. Remember your vows. You promised to comfort, being sensitive and supportive when your spouse is hurting.

Honor each other. To hold each other in highest esteem helps to protect you from destructive power struggles that divide many couples. Husband, you honor her by treasuring her as your most valued asset, recognizing her accomplishments, speaking to her with respect, and helping with household duties. Wife, you honor your husband when you consider and understand his responsibilities, focus on his strengths rather than his weaknesses, communicate appreciation for his efforts, and discover how you can please him.

Keep each other. This is the concept of continuing to belong to each other in a permanent union through the good and bad seasons. When something is given to you for keeps, it really belongs to you. Keeping involves an unswerving loyalty and an active, pursuing love that will not let go. Your spouse is given to you by God and is yours in a very special way – for keeps!

Let's Talk About It

1. Are there any challenges to your marital vows that you want to address?

2. How have the promises you made to each other helped you build a healthy relationship?

3. How can your spouse pray for you now and in the coming week?

Prayer

Heavenly Father, protect and preserve our marriage. Remind us of our promise to love, comfort, honor, and keep each other as long as we both shall live. Do not allow sin, difficulties, or other people to separate what you have joined together.

(Record any insights and decisions in the Journal section.)

Devotional Date #47

Finally, brothers and sisters, whatever is true, whatever is noble, whatever is right, whatever is pure, whatever is lovely, whatever is admirable—if anything is excellent or praiseworthy—think about such things.

Philippians 4:8

. . . .

Your relationship is in trouble when your perception of what your spouse just said is worse than reality. The couples I meet in their season of conflict tend to interpret their spouse's behavior much more negatively than originally intended. It is critical for them to concede the possibility that their negative interpretation could be unfair in some areas.

Scott Stanley's research with marital couples reveals that people tend to see what they expect to see in others. This kind of expectation becomes a filter that colors what we see and distorts communication. Studies also show that our expectations can influence the behavior of others. For example, if you believe that your spouse is mad at you, she may well sound mad when talking with you, even if she isn't. We tend to pull from others the behavior that is consistent with what we expect. Negative interpretations can make things seem a lot worse than they really are.

Negative interpretations are a good example of mind reading – when you assume you know what your spouse is thinking or why he/she did something. When your mind reading includes negative judgments about the thoughts and motives of the other person, you may be in real trouble, both in your marriage and spiritually.

Most actions of our spouses that aggravate us are usually done with the best of intentions or no intentions at all. Your marriage is headed for big trouble when innocent actions of either spouse are consistently interpreted negatively and unfairly. How can you address the negative interpretations in your marriage? Scott Stanley, writing in *A Lasting Promise,* suggests the following action plan:

1. Reconsider what you think is true about some of your spouse's motives. They may be much more positive than you have believed or at least less negative. Only you can control how you interpret your spouse's behavior.

2. Look for evidence that is contrary to the negative interpretation you usually take. If you believe your spouse is uncaring and generally see him/her in that light, then you need to look for evidence to the contrary. Does he/she do some things for you that you like? Could it be that he/she does nice things because he/she cares enough to try to keep the relationship strong?

3. Be willing to give your spouse the benefit of the doubt in wanting to make things better.

Do not allow inaccurate interpretations to sabotage the good you are accomplishing in building a great marriage.

Let's Talk About It

1. When are you more likely to interpret your spouse's words or actions in a negative fashion? What can help you avoid it?

2. How can your spouse pray for you now and in the coming week?

Prayer

Heavenly Father, we do not like it when we do things that make our marriage weak and insecure. Please forgive us for our negative attitudes and interpretations. Fill our hearts with a lasting and understanding love for each other.

(Record any insights and decisions in the Journal section.)

Devotional Date #48

Watch your words and hold your tongue; you'll save yourself a lot of grief.
Proverbs 21:23 (THE MESSAGE)

. . . .

It is not necessary, nor is it wise, to say everything you are thinking. As Solomon's wisdom in Proverbs 21:23 notes, "you'll save yourself a lot of grief." Stop and think – this is key! So many of our communication problems would go away if we formed the discipline of thinking before we speak.

I find that I can save myself a lot of heartache if I *THINK* about the following questions:

- ▪ *Truth – Is it true?* Do not say anything unless you know it is true. When communication gets tough, you have to speak the truth. Stop and think, is this true? Can you validate it with facts?

- ▪ *Helpful – Is it helpful?* Not only is it true, but will it help your spouse and your marriage? Does it add value to the conversation or does it just get you both sidetracked? Is this the right time and place to share what is on your mind?

- ▪ *Inspiring – Is it inspiring?* When you get loose with your tongue in the heated moments of communication, trouble is at hand. Will your words be encouraging or only serve to advance your own agenda?

- ▪ *Necessary – Is it necessary?* Discipline in communication means knowing what to say and when to say it. Solomon wrote that there is "a time to be quiet and a time to speak up" (Ecclesiastes 3:7, NLT). Not everything you think between your ears needs to come out of your mouth. A piece of wisdom I picked up in my marital journey is this: Never miss an opportunity to keep your mouth shut.

- **Kind** – *Can I say it in a kind way?* Some people believe you have to tell your spouse everything. Others believe that being kind means some things are left unspoken. If you have a choice between being right and being kind, always choose to be kind. I am not suggesting you avoid the difficult conversations that may be required. Simply take the time to check your heart and attitude. Can you say it in a kind way? When you are tempted to say unkind things, you might make a practice of saying something like, "Right now I am frustrated. I want to wait until I'm feeling better to make any requests and suggestions."

Let's Talk About It

1. Why do you think couples have difficulty speaking in kind ways about difficult topics in their marriage?

2. How does the *THINK* material apply to your relationship?

3. How can your spouse pray for you now and in the coming week?

Prayer

Heavenly Father, help us discern when and how to deal with the difficult topics in our marriage. May our words be true, helpful, inspiring, necessary, and kind.

(Record any insights and decisions in the Journal section.)

Devotional Date #49

The Lord is faithful, and he will strengthen and protect you from the evil one.

2 Thessalonians 3:3

. . . .

Most people desire a happy and long-lasting marriage. They enter marriage with the strong desire and determination for a loving partnership.

However, too many couples find that goal eluding them. According to David & Claudia Arp, award-winning authors of the *10 Great Dates* series, these couples are not well prepared to handle some key threats to a healthy marriage relationship. What are those threats?

Marital grudges and disappointments will sabotage a couple's ability to build a stronger bond. Unrealistic and unmet expectations contribute to these grudges. Realizing your spouse will never change can have a negative influence on your attitude about the state of your marriage. A lack of forgiveness will result in disappointment, inappropriate anger, and negative feelings towards your spouse. It is important to keep short accounts with each other, deal with conflicts quickly, and focus on grace in your marriage.

Ineffective and unproductive communication patterns prevent the clear sharing of your deepest feelings, joys, and concerns. Stonewalling, defensiveness, and constant criticism rob a marriage of its growing intimacy and its ability to navigate difficult waters. To counter this threat, you will do well to learn how to discuss problems and resolve conflicts without destroying each other.

Boredom and emotional separation can creep into your hearts before you know it. You become comfortable with each other. You take each other for granted. You fail to maintain the little acts of caring and kindness that invigorate the friendship aspect of your marriage. You can also lose interest in romance and sexual intimacy. Couples in healthy marriages are not satisfied with a "good enough" marriage.

Changing roles and responsibilities can throw you off balance. As children get older and become more independent, you may not be able to adapt, especially if your sense of personal value is derived largely from a life revolving around your children. Instead of adjusting for the sake of the marriage, some people cling to defined marital roles that are now ineffective. This can happen when a major illness strikes either one or both of you. Everything changes when there is a chronic illness or disability. Flexibility is a fundamental ingredient for a lasting marriage.

Many problems can cripple or fatally wound a marriage. The issues in today's Devotional Date do not have to destroy the harmony and joy of your marriage. They will, however, if you do not protect your marriage from them.

Let's Talk About It

1. Has boredom crept into your marriage? Explain.

2. How are you protecting your marriage from these threats? What more can you do?

3. How can your spouse pray for you now and in the coming week?

Prayer

Heavenly Father, we thank you for the promise of your abiding presence in our lives. Protect our marriage from the things that threaten our unity and love. We ask you to give us courage to forgive quickly and to be flexible when necessary. As we go through the years ahead of us, we trust in your promise that you will never leave or forsake us.

(Record any insights and decisions in the Journal section.)

Devotional Date #50

Do not deprive each other of sexual relations, unless you both agree to refrain from sexual intimacy for a limited time so you can give yourselves more completely to prayer. Afterward, you should come together again so that Satan won't be able to tempt you because of your lack of self-control.

1 Corinthians 7:5 (NLT)

. . . .

A great lover in a great marriage is a disciplined lover. Discipline may seem like an odd character trait, the opposite of playful and spontaneous. However, a lack of opportunity and priority sabotages the spontaneity of many married couples. Here are several ways in which you can be disciplined in your love life:

Make sexual intimacy a priority. This starts with a positive attitude about sex and the determination to prevent the "stuff of life" from crowding in on this vital area of married life. Give your best time and energy to this important part of your marriage.

Plan for sexual activity with your spouse. You may even have to put it on your calendars! You can then allow for spontaneity in the atmosphere, place, timing, and technique.

Take care of your body and mind. Good physical, mental, and emotional health empower your lovemaking.

Say "yes" more frequently. Saying "no" can become a habit that prolongs sexual dissatisfaction. When you are tired or you just do not feel like it, go ahead and take the plunge. Many have reported they were glad they did.

Structure your life in such a way that you can be rested, rather than tired. Take a nap in the afternoon or go to bed earlier at night. Maybe you need to reclaim some time on your calendar because you are overcommitted.

Plan uninterrupted times together where you are free from the stress and distractions of family and work. Couples who have children at home will greatly benefit from such times. Arrange for grandparents or friends to take care of your children, while you have a special overnight at a nearby hotel (or at your empty house).

Be creative in your love life. Initiate lovemaking at unexpected times and in unexpected places. Try new positions and techniques. You might even try being the "initiator" if your spouse usually gets things started.

Read a book together about how to have a healthy sexual relationship. Kevin Leman's book, *Sheet Music,* is a great resource and a fun read.

Take more time to enjoy the lovemaking. It does not have to be a race against the clock. For many people, that means going to bed earlier.

Ask God to bless your love life. He is very interested in helping you create a life of passion, joy, and satisfaction. Because of your inherent differences, you need God's grace to create a fulfilling intimate relationship.

The investment of time and energy in your love life will yield high dividends. You will feel closer, more relaxed, more connected, and more married.

Let's Talk About It

1. Reviewing the list above, which ones are present in your marriage?

2. What one thing can you do in the next month to show your spouse that you want to make your love life a priority?

3. How can your spouse pray for you now and in the coming week?

Prayer

Heavenly Father, give us a hunger and desire for each other that is holy and pure in every way. May our love life be blessed by you and fully satisfying for us.

(Record any insights and decisions in the Journal section.)

Devotional Date #51

Since they are no longer two but one, let no one separate them,
for God has joined them together.

Matthew 19:6 (NLT)

. . . .

It was a hot, hazy, and humid summer day. I walked to the Post Office to buy some stamps. Placing them in my shirt pocket, I continued through my daily routine. At the end of the day, I discovered that the two layers of stamps in the booklet had stuck together. This was back in the days when postage stamps required you to moisten the glue on them before applying them to the envelope.

Since they were apparently useless to me, I returned them to the Post Office, requesting an exchange, only to discover that "all sales are final." How was I to use them? The clerk obviously had confronted this dilemma with other customers. He peeled back one corner of the bonded strips, then swiftly separated the two layers of stamps. Handing the book of stamps back to me, he wished me a good day. "Are they still usable?" I asked. "Of course," he said.

I have long remembered that day, reflecting on the similarity between what God says about marriage and the bonding of those stamps. You see, those two layers of stamps had become one. They bonded in much the same way God has designed the marriage relationship.

What I saw after the tearing apart of the two layers reminded me that divorce leaves its mark on all involved. As the two layers were pulled apart, ink spots from the printed side of the second layer remained on the sticky underside of the top layer. I realized that as those stamps traveled along wherever we sent the envelopes, they carried the impact and imprint of that bonding experience.

Such is the power of the bond that takes place in marriage. We are no longer two, but one. Tear us apart and we carry the influence of that bonding experience into future relationships.

Unity and oneness in marriage is not automatic. It is the result of discipline, determination, and hard work. It is an uncompromising commitment to a marriage that honors God's presence in your lives and one that you want your children to duplicate. By following God's design for marriage, you can build a marriage that will survive and thrive in the midst of life's challenges.

Let's Talk About It

1. In what ways is your marital bond strong? Weak?

2. What are three things you can do in the coming week to fortify your marital unity?

3. How can your spouse pray for you now and in the coming week?

Prayer

Heavenly Father, give us strength to overcome all of the difficulties that we are dealing with now and protect us against all problems we may encounter in the future. May the love that binds us grow stronger as we fulfill the destiny you have laid out for us.

(Record any insights and decisions in the Journal section.)

Devotional Date #52

May he give you the desire of your heart and make all your plans succeed.

Psalm 20:4

. . . .

Over the years, I have noticed a similarity between the way people take care of their marriages and the way they take care of their cars and trucks.

They do nothing and break down. There are people who ignore the preventative maintenance schedule of their automobiles. They disregard the odd rumbling sounds coming from underneath. They are convinced that they have an adequate fuel supply, regardless of what the gas gauge says. Eventually, they break down by the side of the road. The same thing can happen to you. You refuse to heed the warnings and lack the motivation or interest in preventing trouble. The next thing you know, your spouse drags you into a counselor's office or a marriage seminar as a means of repairing the problem. This is often costly, as it is when we neglect to take care of our vehicles. Years of neglect will require major changes in behavior and attitude.

They wait until they get a warning ticket due to some defect. They just keep going about their own agendas until something happens to get their attention. It may be an argument that leads to abuse, or a narrow escape from a sexual temptation, or a health-related issue that causes them to refocus their priorities. While not ideal, couples who wait until they get a warning ticket will often seek help. They will talk to a pastor or return to the positive patterns of relating. Others will attend a marriage class or seminar to stabilize their relationship.

They follow a preventative maintenance schedule. Like those who zealously perform the preventative maintenance rituals upon their cars, these couples focus creative energy on their marriage as a means of preventing trouble. A husband told me that for 30 years he changed his car's oil regularly, kept the tire pressure at factory specifications, and maintained the various fluid levels according to the owner's manual. After attending one of our marriage seminars, he realized he had neglected to keep his marriage running smoothly through regular check-ups. With a little preventative maintenance, you can save yourself a huge chunk of time and emotional energy trying to repair a big problem later on. It can make your marriage run smoother and be more fun in the years ahead. Couples who take this path have intentional discussions about the health of their marriage, read books together on how to improve communication, spend time having fun, and attend marriage enrichment events.

Your marriage is probably a good marriage, but it can be stronger. A preventive maintenance plan will help you build a great marriage.

Let's Talk About It

1. Discuss your thoughts on why married couples fail to take care of their relationship.

2. What will you do or continue to do in the coming year(s) to prevent a breakdown in your marriage?

3. How can your spouse pray for you now and in the coming week?

Prayer

Heavenly Father, thank you for our marriage and for the love we share. Help us to build our lives and marriage on your truth so we can stand strong in your divine plan for us. May our love for each other never fail.

(Record any insights and decisions in the Journal section.)

Devotional Date
Journal

Use this Journal section to record your insights and decisions from your Devotional Dates. This will help you stay focused on what God is saying to you about your marriage. You will also find it encouraging as you review it in the years to come.

Journal

_____

_____

_____

_____

_____

_____

_____

_____

_____

_____

_____

_____

_____

_____

_____

_____

_____

_____

Journal

Journal

_____

_____

_____

_____

_____

_____

_____

_____

_____

_____

_____

_____

_____

_____

_____

_____

_____

_____

Journal

_____

_____

_____

_____

_____

_____

_____

_____

_____

_____

_____

_____

_____

_____

_____

_____

Journal

_____

_____

_____

_____

_____

_____

_____

_____

_____

_____

_____

_____

_____

_____

Journal

_____

_____

_____

_____

_____

_____

_____

_____

_____

_____

_____

_____

_____

_____

_____

_____

Journal

_____

_____

_____

_____

_____

_____

_____

_____

_____

_____

_____

_____

_____

_____

_____

_____

Journal

Journal

_____

_____

_____

_____

_____

_____

_____

_____

_____

_____

_____

_____

_____

_____

_____

_____

_____

_____

Journal

_____

_____

_____

_____

_____

_____

_____

_____

_____

_____

_____

_____

_____

_____

_____

_____

_____

_____

_____

Journal

_____

_____

_____

_____

_____

_____

_____

_____

_____

_____

_____

_____

_____

_____

_____

_____

Journal

_____

_____

_____

_____

_____

_____

_____

_____

_____

_____

_____

_____

_____

_____

_____

_____

_____

Journal

_____

_____

_____

_____

_____

_____

_____

_____

_____

_____

_____

_____

_____

_____

_____

_____

Journal

_____

_____

_____

_____

_____

_____

_____

_____

_____

_____

_____

_____

_____

_____

_____

_____

_____

_____

Journal

_____

_____

_____

_____

_____

_____

_____

_____

_____

_____

_____

_____

_____

_____

_____

_____

_____

_____

About the Author

William *"Willie"* Batson is an engaging presenter who speaks nationally with authority on today's family relationships. He inspires his audiences with practical instruction that challenges couples and parents to work together through relational issues with a Christ-centered approach. Willie brings both humor and practical wisdom to his presentations. His work genuinely reflects a calling from God in his life.

Willie and Cindy met at a Christian college in New England and married in 1972. They are the parents of two married daughters and are extremely proud to claim six grandchildren as their own.

Founder of Family Builders Ministries in 1987, Willie served as its President until retiring in 2017 to focus on caring for Cindy as she fought the progression of her chronic illness. Cindy passed away in February 2018 from complications related to Multiple Sclerosis, a debilitating disease she battled for 27 years.

Willie is an ordained pastor with a degree in theology from Berkshire Christian College and a Master of Arts in Family Ministry from Gordon-Conwell Theological Seminary. He has served churches in South Carolina, Connecticut, New Hampshire, and Maine.

A published author, Willie wrote his first book, *Tools for a Great Marriage*, in 2008. It has enjoyed worldwide distribution and gained acclaim from readers and noted authors such as Dr. Gary Chapman (*The Five Love Languages*) and David & Claudia Arp (*10 Great Dates* series).

Willie is available to speak at churches and conferences on topics that can help people build great relationships.

For more information about Willie's current ministry and to schedule him to speak at your church or event, visit his website:
www.williebatson.com

Having equipped engaged and married couples for more than 45 years, Willie Batson has written a book containing marital tools that can help any couple build a satisfying and lasting relationship. "Couples enter marriage with their own bag of tools," says Willie, "but are frustrated by their attempts at fixing things. They either have the wrong tools or do not use the tools properly." Having the right tools in your marital tool bag can help you build and sustain a great marriage.

In *Tools for a Great Marriage,* couples learn how to...

- Turn their bad talk into love talk.

- Make their personality differences work for them.

- Practice the *Principle of Satisfaction* in their sex life.

- Defeat the enemy of every marriage – selfishness.

- Turn stormy times into opportunities to love each other more.

- Keep conflicts from turning into nasty, knockdown, drag-out fights.

"...you will discover not only the tools, but also the knowledge of how to use those tools to build a great marriage. The dreams you had when you said, 'I do,' can become reality when you apply these insights."

- Dr. Gary Chapman, author of *The Five Love Languages*

"My husband and I wish we had known about these easy to use tools when we were first married. You will find that they can make an incredible difference in your marriage. Don't wait until your marriage is in trouble. Start now to build a great marriage!"

Tools for a Great Marriage is available online at
www.williebatson.com and www.Amazon.com

Made in the USA
Middletown, DE
21 September 2021

48766033R00076